C000116144

Town plan, 1908.

Bygone
ROMFORD

The *King's Arms* yard in 1887.

Bygone
ROMFORD

Brian Evans

Phillimore

1988

Published by
PHILLIMORE & CO. LTD.
Shopwyke Hall, Chichester, Sussex

© Brian Evans, 1988

ISBN 0 85033 659 6

Printed and bound by
BIDDLES LTD.
Guildford, Surrey

List of Illustrations

Acknowledgements
The author would like to thank Mrs. J. Franklin, E. N. Green, Mr. Harris, Havering Libraries, Vernon Hood, Passmore Edwards Museum, Irvan Radford, Romford Historical Society and Roy Squire for the loan of photographs; Larry Morgan, Irvan Radford, Roy Squire and T. & B. Photographic for reproduction of photographs; and Irvan Radford for 'rescuing' plates 9, 10, 14, 15, 16a & b and 69, and for information on the Georgian buildings in the Market Place. The author apologises for any omissions in these acknowledgements – several versions exist of prints taken from glass plate negatives and it is not always known who holds the original.

Introduction

A Long Time Growing

Over many centuries Romford, though always an attraction to people from many miles around because of its market and meeting places, had itself grown very little. Called a town from very early times because of its connection with the Royal Palace and its central position on the Great Road between London and East Anglia, it was nevertheless still basically a village and remained as such until the 20th century. All this time, as we are frequently reminded by writers in the 17th, 18th and 19th centuries, it consisted principally of one long street, the main buildings abutting on the through road which was bisected at the *Golden Lion* junction by roads leading north and south.

The earliest settlement was probably in a clearing in the woods which, because of the swampy nature of the Rom basin, hugged the slightly higher ground towards Heath Park. The first inhabitants probably came by boat along the river, having navigated through the woods fringing the bank, from the Thames. They settled here because of the promising sheltered aspect of the terrain. Later, the Romans passed through, building their great strategic road and founding *Durolitum*. This may have been located in the Hare Street/ Gidea Park area. Interestingly Hare Street may derive its name from the Saxon word for army. *Durolitum* was a strategic military posting station rather than a fully fledged town. This is suggested by its position between larger centres, guarding the ways east-west and north-south and the Rom crossing. Other scattered Roman sites in the vicinity may have been spawned by the Great Road. A burial pot discovered while the Dolphin Leisure Centre was being built indicates a Roman cemetery on this spot very close to the main road. Other finds in the wider area include a villa at Collier Row and remains at Rainham.

Judging from the extant documents, recording the buying and selling and transfer of land and property in medieval times, Romford enjoyed several 'boom' periods when it became a popular and convenient place to live and much sought after as a business centre. The original site at Oldchurch was frequently flooded in early medieval days and the church was therefore rebuilt on the higher ground by the Great Road. Other important activities like trading and administration followed the priests to what is now the market place. The presence of the Royal Palace at Havering-atte-Bower village, only a few miles to the north, gave a further boost to the town's vitality. Many important people from London acquired the large houses and estates in the vicinity and many new houses were built in the town in the 16th, 17th and 18th centuries. The 1984 archaeological excavation at the far end of the market place revealed 18th-century housing occupying a site formerly containing a tannery. Items found in the remains of the row of brick and timber houses reveal a surprising wealth of luxury goods such as Venetian glass, Chinese porcelain and Dutch, German and Spanish pottery. In late 18th-century directories of Romford there are surprisingly fashionable trades listed – milliners, perfumers, wine-merchants and umbrella makers among them and these continue into the early 19th-century lists. In the middle and late 19th century, after the arrival of the railway, Romford burgeoned as a shopping centre. This commercial growth is typified in success stories like that of Denny Stone who set up a small shop on very little capital, but lived to see his business grow and take over more and more premises. In the lifetime of his children it became a large department store.

The early 19th-century 'fashionable' atmosphere in the town may have been encouraged by the great number of coaches which passed through the town, some forty daily for various destinations. There was also a great deal of money to be made supplying the London market with food and provisions, for anybody with capital to invest in land. The leather industry produced locally every kind of leather article including leather breeches for which Romford had long become famous in proverb. The cattle market made the town the 'capital' of the surrounding area, though Romford did not increase in size to any extent. It was not until the railway arrived on its high bank in 1839 that new streets began to be laid out and areas to the immediate west of the town started to fill with housing. At first only a few estates were developed outside the nucleus. Later and particularly after the First World War the great expansion between Romford and its neighbouring towns and villages took place. Up to the Second World War and indeed since, this growth of housing and commercial development has been unceasing, sweeping away the remains of buildings from earlier centuries and obliterating much of the uniqueness of Romford as a locality.

Romford Market – A Meeting Place

Like most centuries-old enclosures, Romford market had its own unique atmosphere. The last cattle sale was held on 21 May 1958, bringing to an end a very long tradition. The market days brought many characters to town along with the farmers and dealers. Among the most interesting were the Welsh drovers who brought cattle over incredible distances on foot. Their secret was to bring the animals in easy stages and to shoe the creatures with pieces of iron, fixed by the drovers themselves. It was said that the drovers had the ability to swear 'frequently, fluently and with expression'.

One erroneous idea about the market which has taken root is that it was set up by charter. In fact this was not necessary. Henry III as the landlord merely ordered the Sheriff of Essex to proclaim publicly throughout the county that the market was to be held and this order was recorded officially in the Close Rolls. The market benefited from all the rights and customs appertaining to such an establishment. The official day laid down in the order was Wednesday. Over the years markets of various kinds have been held on other days. A 1769 description gives the following: 'It has two markets, that on Tuesday is for hogs, calves, and other cattle; and that on Wednesdays for corn', while in the *Universal British Directory* of 1798, Romford 'has three markets weekly, viz. Monday for hogs; Tuesday for calves, sheep and lambs; and Wednesday for corn, cattle, horses, sheep, hogs, lambs, poultry and butchers' meat'.

The market was not just a buying and selling place, but a venue which could be used for news gathering, information for consumers, tips for crop growing, as a kind of debating place and a place to receive medical attention. All of these and many other activities took place in the inns and shops and other houses lining the boundaries of the great plain. For instance in the *Chelmsford Chronicle* for 5 June 1840 there is an advertisement:

Dr. Rees, 8 Craven Street, Strand, London and New Cross, Deptford, Kent, informs his patients in Essex that he attends every Wednesday at the Dolphin Inn, Romford, Essex, from 10 to 1 o' clock where he may be consulted in all inward complaints. Consumption and Liver Complaints successfully treated by Dr. Rees after the experience of 40 years.

In the same journal for 3 July, a Mr. Thompson who describes himself as a Surgeon Dentist announces he will be in attendance every Wednesday at Mr. Braby's, next to the *Dolphin* from 11 to 4 o' clock. He sets his prospectus out as follows:

Artificial teeth fixed upon the most approved principles, from a single tooth to a whole set without extracting roots, or giving any pain whatsoever, rendering it impossible to distinguish them from the natural ones, and answering all the purposes of Articulation and Mastication. All operations on the teeth and gums judiciously performed – Consultations free.

Quite a promise, considering the year was only 1840.

Eleven public houses are mentioned in the pictorial survey of the market. A twelfth, the *Lamb*, is mentioned elsewhere and still exists, although it was rebuilt after a fire in 1852. The *Cock and Bell* no longer trades as a public house but the building is still there and is the oldest one in the market. This building has had a colourful history. It was constructed as a private house by a certain John Atte Street. It passed to another John – John Atte Downes – after whom the house became known as 'Downes', still during the late 15th century, shortly after it had been built. In the year 1480 a courtier of Henry VII of the picturesque name of Avery Cornburgh endowed a Chantry by buying this house, conveniently standing next to the church. In the house which now became known as 'the Preestes Chambre' were installed a priest and two assistants or clerks. These were responsible for saying masses for the souls of Cornburgh, his wife, his sister and his chaplain Dr. John Cowland. Rich and important people of the time were very aware in an age when life was much shorter that provision for the safety of their souls had to be made at an early stage. The house is thought to have remained as a Chantry until 1547 when 'all these superstitious customs' were abolished. Next, two speculators, Richard Venables and John Maynerde, bought the property and others associated with it, in 1549. By 1613 the house had come into the possession of the Grafton family and was an inn named the *Cock and Bell*, under which sign it remained until closed down in 1908. When the mail coaches began in 1785, the Norwich coach made its first stop from London at the *Cock and Bell*. The horses and mail were exchanged and all of Romford would have heard the post horn as the mail swung away across the market, the horn warning the tollgate man to open the gate. The mailcoaches were noted for their accurate timekeeping and did not have time to waste.

Romford's first recorded postmaster is Mr. Spicer of 1672. In about 1830 a Mr. Attwell was appointed. He was the owner of a fancy bazaar in the market place. He was also an agent for the Essex Economic Insurance Co. and sold newspapers. In 1848 he is listed as William Henry Attwell, postmaster, and the post for London had to be at his office by 8.45 a.m. and 3.45 p.m. Previous postmasters operating from the market place were Roger Barton in 1811 and William Warwick in 1823. The office later transferred to the High Street and then to various locations in South Street.

Many great occasions were celebrated in the market place such as the 1918 signing of the Armistice when a haycart loaded high with straw and hay was pulled onto the cobbles and a victory bonfire lit. There were religious meetings, election junketings as well as parades by the Scouts. On more than one occasion a wife was sold in the market. In 1832 for instance:

A good-looking young woman, wife of Thomas Newcombe, to whom she had been married only one month, was last week brought to Romford Market in a halter, and sold by public auction for 5s. 6d., with the addition of 6d. for the new rope by which she was tied to the post. In this sale the customary fees were discharged – viz. Toll, two pence; Pitching, three pence.

It is believed by one writer that this alternative to divorce was practised more widely than hitherto realised and lasted for 500 years in Britain.

South Street – from Trackway to Shopping Mecca

South Street probably began its career as a trackway parallel to the River Rom. When the early medieval town was wetting its feet by the frequently overflowing river at Oldchurch, this track connected the low ground here with the rising ground of Heath Park and Squirrels Heath via other paths leading eastward. To the north it met the old Roman highway, near the present market place, then quite a wooded district. Going south it travelled across the marshes to Rainham. A final connection was with the ancient east-west thoroughfare or green lane running from the Ilford direction. This had been the equivalent of a pre-Roman highway probably dating from ancient British times and still in existence in one form or another in Roman and Saxon days. Old Romford at Oldchurch lay along the path of this green lane. Today the Ilford end of its route is still marked by the road named Green Lane, running towards Becontree Heath.

Up to the 19th century Hornchurch Lane, as South Street was then called, remained a backwater. This can be seen from the Crawter survey of 1812. Only one side of the lane is shown, but it was clearly very rural, the only buildings being at the market end. The one substantial structure was the mansion house of the Manor of Stewards. The lands of this estate stretched all the way down the east side of South Street with a western extension to include the 'ruin fields' at Oldchurch, and reached as far as Squirrel's Heath. Holgate's survey of the manor gives a unique glimpse of part of Romford in about 1696, when all major activity was concentrated in the market area, with farmland around South Street. Just above Stewards in the street were the properties whose rents endowed the Charity School. Stewards was afterwards taken down and a new building known as Romford Hall constructed. This, with its less extensive grounds, still gave the upper part of South Street a rural appearance, right into the 20th century, with trees peeping over a brick wall.

One of the fascinating features of the 1812 plan is the depiction of the post mill which lay behind the present *Morland Arms*. A short length of alleyway which once served the mill still connects South Street with Victoria Road. Afterwards Whitmore's Steam Mills occupied an extended site at the bottom end of Victoria Road. The name Old Mill Parade on a line of shops commemorates this.

It was the coming of the railway that altered South Street. As soon as the railway was opened on 18 June 1839, the street began to awake from its long slumber. Above the station, a County Court was in place by 1854. Later, in 1894, the police station moved from its old premises in the court house, market place, to a building on the west side of the street, facing the court. Eastern, Western and Junction Roads were developed on land to the east of the street as an early result of the railway service. Gradually as the town moved into the 20th century, the remaining private houses in the thoroughfare above the railway were converted into shops. By the 1930s it had become the 'Golden Mile', Romford's most popular and fashionable shopping street with four cinemas located here at various times and two covered shopping arcades. One of these, simply known as 'the Arcade' and facing the Western Road Corner, has surprisingly been redeveloped. The other, the Quadrant Arcade, still continues in refurbished form.

Transport and Travel

Romford was put on the travel map of Britain by the building of the great Roman road between London, Chelmsford and Colchester. The actual documentary record for this exists in the Roman road book, the Antonine Itinerary, in which *Durolitum* is listed as a place 15 Roman miles from London. This would locate it in the area of Gidea Park, formerly known as Hare Street, where the *Ship Inn* stands on an old site facing the centuries old thoroughfare. *Durolitum* is likely to have been little more than a posting station where fresh horses were kept for travellers on the road. There may also have been a strategic barracks from which soldiers could be dispatched to any required point in the region. It would have been a wise precaution to guard this remote, wooded route along which ambushes could be mounted. The natives may have been conquered but they were not always quiescent as Boudicca proved.

After the Romans abandoned Britain in A.D. 410, the road for some centuries became an even more dangerous place. Many tribes from the Continent invaded Britain, particularly this corner of the land which the Saxon shore forts no longer guarded. When the Saxons themselves began to settle they in turn found themselves vulnerable to Danes and other marauders. The Saxons therefore built their villages off the main roads, either to the south or north of the highway. Ilford, Romford and Brentwood were all originally sited in this way and it was not until medieval times that Romford began to re-align itself along the highway. The roads however remained in a bad state through manorial times, although the lord sometimes got his tenants to put in some repair work. In 1555 a new Act of Parliament made road improvement the responsibility of the parish. Each had to appoint an unpaid Surveyor of Highways for a year at a time. He had to supervise the parishioners who were to provide tools, carts, materials and labour for eight hours on four days of the year (later increased to six). It proved difficult to enforce these provisions and such an amateur workforce was unlikely to effect any dramatic improvement. Travel remained slow and uncomfortable until after 1706 when control of such important stretches of road as the London-Colchester highway was transferred to various Turnpike Trusts under Acts of Parliament. The trustees, usually prominent locals, were empowered to collect tolls and apply the resulting funds to repair and improve the road. Once this system got into its stride, the great age of coaching began and lasted until the railways appeared in the mid-19th century. These were prosperous times for Romford. Many of the inns in the town had capacious yards and stabling from years of serving the traveller's needs. Forty coaches to and from London pulled up at one of the Romford inns such as the *White Hart, King's Head* or *Dolphin* each weekday. Other long distance coaches from Cambridge and Norwich drove straight through. Carriers of goods and local coaches also made their way to London several times a week.

The great number of coaches and private carriages on the lonely stretches of highway began to attract highwaymen and footpads. In 1769 for instance the following robbery is recorded in a newspaper: 'Thursday Morning last, about Seven o'Clock, the Norwich Post-Coach was stopped near Rumford Gallows, by a young highwayman, extremely well-mounted, who robbed one of the inside Passengers of Two Guineas, and the other of about Thirty Shillings. His Hand trembled while he held the pistol, but he behaved with the greatest Politeness'. In the same year another report reads: 'On Wednesday Evening, about 7 o'Clock, Mr. Baines of Newport Market, was knocked down by two footpads near the Whalebone at Rumford and robbed of Two Guineas and his Watch'. Mugging is not a new activity!

The opening of the railway through to Brentwood on 1 July 1840, and eventually to Colchester, did tend to empty the main roads. However some short distance road travel was stimulated by the need to connect the early railheads with the smaller villages. Thus Romford station had connecting road coaches to Hornchurch, Upminster and Ockendon in 1840 and these lasted for some years until these villages gained their own railway line to London. A local coach from Romford continued to run until 1859 on the London road, with return trips twice a day. Many of the older people, not being used to the trains, refused to travel to London except by coach for many years after the advent of the iron road. It was a shilling outside and 18d. inside for the journey from the *White Hart* at Romford (now the *Bitter End*) to the *Goose and Gridiron* public house near St Paul's in London. The coach carried 16 outside and 12 inside passengers.

Romford was fortunate that, when the railway station was opened in 1839, it was situated in the town centre. However, the station was rather inadequately built on its embankment and the small bridges over the roads prevented widening of the track. Until this was remedied by a costly scheme at the beginning of the 1930s, heavier traffic on the line was impossible. This again gave road traffic, in the form of buses, a competitive edge when Romford's rapid shopping and housing development began after the First World War.

North Street and Mawney's

In 1890, North Street was still very much an old world byeway leading out of the town, consisting of a rambling collection of wooden and plaster-fronted buildings dating from various centuries. One entered the street through the footway from the crossroads at the centre of Romford, with the overhanging storey of the *Golden Lion* just above. When vehicles still shared this entrance with pedestrians, it appeared dangerously inadequate. In fact there was no footway on the right hand side until a later date. Several buildings of interest were visible just beyond the end of the *Golden Lion* range of outhouses. Most important, from the fact that this was the road to the Royal Palace at Havering Village, was the mansion known as Canons. This lay on the right hand side just below Church Lane and was believed to have housed the majority of the royal servants on duty at the palace. These had to be augmented when a royal visit was planned as there was always much work to do to bring the rural retreat up to standard. The alternative name of this house was 'the Familiarum'. In 1908 the venerable building, which had been refronted in Georgian times though still retaining its ancient interior, was split into two dwellings. This building lingered on into the 1940s and '50s but was eventually demolished in the days before public awareness of the need for architectural conservation was so great.

A little further up, on the left of the street, stood the quaint Roger Reede almshouses, still on their original site, although they had been rebuilt on several occasions since their foundation in 1452. Still further up on the right hand pavement was the *Northern Star* public house in old premises which survive in the main although the inn was closed in 1898 and the licence transferred to the *Mawney Arms* when the fields of Mawney's manor were being developed into roads.

Building over the Mawney's Estate began in 1883 when the old *Woolpack* public house in the High Street was demolished to clear the way for a new road, right over the old fields through to Prospect Place on the Collier Row Lane extension of North Street. This was Mawney's Road – the last 's' was later dropped. The original entrance to the farmland and fields of Mawney's manor, indeed the only entrance for hundreds of years, lay slightly to the west along the High Street. Mawney's Lane led to footpaths across the fields. If these were followed, Marks Gate on the far western boundary of the Romford district was eventually reached. Later the construction of Eastern Avenue across the meadows in the 1920s cut the northern remainder of this fieldpath in two, although it still exists as a right of way. The short length of Mawney's Lane was lined with picturesque wooden-fronted cottages, though their sanitary arrangements left something to be desired.

Returning to North Street, opposite the *Northern Star* was Como Street which extended only a short distance westwards until the opening up of Mawney's for building. Just above Como Street, Stickleback Lane ran down towards the little plank bridge across the River Rom and the fields of Brooklands on the other side. Above this area, North Street soon became a country lane with only the occasional building, the road winding between hedges uphill to Havering village. Marshalls Estate on the left hand side, it is true, sported a brick wall along its length, which was sometimes breached by the stream flooding near the present *Parkside* public house which had not then been built.

Hainault Road forked to the left from North Street at this point and the average Romfordian thought of this area as being the back of beyond. Hainault Road probably earned this reputation because Gale's brickyard lay along one side. This meant that development of the manor of East House (as it had been) proceeded very slowly. There were still breaks in the roads and even stiles to climb over. Milk was fetched from a farmhouse behind Prospect Cottages, adding the final rural touch to the scene.

High Street and West Side of the Town

Apart from the market, the High Street was the most densely built up part of old Romford, being the western part of the 'one long street', a phrase used to describe the town in the early 19th century. One of the older buildings, which has survived several demolition threats, dominates the north-east corner. This is the *Golden Lion* which can trace its ancestry back to before 1440 when it was called simply *The Lion*. The oldest part of the present structure is probably of 16th-century date. Opposite the *Lion*, on the corner of South Street, was an ancient inn known as the *Crown* early in the last century. When it was closed, it was taken over as a chemist's which later became Lasham's well-known business. Lasham's son rebuilt his premises at the end of the century, creating a much taller architect-designed frontage.

Looking along the north side of the street beyond the *Lion* just before the First World War, one would see the substantial but plain front of the Corn Exchange and then a plethora of shops cheek by jowl in the narrow street with its inadequate footway. These included Pearson's the jeweller, Pink's the ironmonger, Dunball's the cycle agent at No. 18, Athur Crewdson (tailor), J. H. Blackwell (butcher), Fletcher's the stationer, Leonard Watts the fishmonger, Henry Meehan (hairdresser) and Porritt's, two shops – a pawnbroker at No. 44 and a furniture dealer at No. 46 High Street, extending round into Mawney's Road at the corner. All these were crammed into a short stretch, not to mention the open bridge parapet or the long frontage of the *Coach and Bell Inn*.

Also tucked away under archways and behind the front premises of the High Street were many yards and courts. These caused concern to the authorities because of the great number of people living in insanitary conditions in close proximity. The General Board of Health report of 1850 found that:

> Ray's square consists of 14 houses, tenanted by 53 persons. There are dwellings on two sides of the court, the surface of which is unpaved and covered with refuse matter of every kind. A large open cesspool is in the centre of the square and near it is the one privy of the place. This is never emptied and the matter that does not pass off by evaporation overflows and settles on the surface of the court. Mr. Potter stated that this had been one of the localities of cholera in 1849 ...

In the years following the report, many of the dwellings were taken down. It was renamed Brazier's Yard and a mission created two halls from three of the remaining houses. The mission helped the needy of the area and provided a badly-needed temperance club for the men. Two public houses on the north side of the street have already been mentioned and along the south side were the *White Hart*, the *White Hart* tap, the Romford Brewery premises and, continuing in the one curving line into London Road, the *New Mill Inn*, the *Compasses* and the *Sun Inn*. In addition, the north side had the *Woolpack* (now the *Angel Hotel*) and the *Romford Arms* at the corner of Mawney's Lane. In addition, all the 13 or so other hostelries in the centre of the town were within easy reach.

One of these other public houses, a rather small one, lay a short way down Waterloo Road. This road was a High Street entrance to what was earlier known as the Barrack Ground, an estate of about 200 cottages which had been constructed on the site of the old cavalry barracks during the days of the Napoleonic invasion scare.

The far west end of town, past the Salem chapel and the windmill, tapered off into the High Road to London. Here was open country, in the late 18th and early 19th century the haunt of highwaymen and footpads. An 1815 account of this part of town stated:

> Passing by Ingrams the baker there is the lane leading to the Old Church. In this lane there is the entry to the Cavalry Barracks as also one in the High Road. Although this is the west end of the town it is the least aristocratic. Collier's mill now presents itself. There is nothing more to be seen except a farm house or two with Tyler's house, Colonel of the Romford Volunteers.

Fire, Flood and Accident

Accidents sometimes occurred on market day in old Romford when animals escaped and ran into shops or injured people. Occasionally animals were themselves injured if they ran out on to the old turnpike road. Around the turn of the century three accidents of a rather more alarming nature occurred.

In March 1894, James Theobald, a popular M.P. for Romford, made a last-minute dash for a departing train and fell between the platform and the moving train. He was taken to the *Golden Lion Inn* where a doctor examined him. He had suffered multiple injuries and died in the early hours of the next day. Then in November 1908 an accident occurred at a building just above the *Bull Inn* in the Market Place, recently acquired by Mr. Jarvis, a well known tailor and clothier. The premises were being extensively rebuilt and one evening collapsed just as children from the Roman Catholic and St Edward's schools were passing on their way home. Seven children were knocked down by the debris but, although some suffered concussion, internal injuries and broken bones, three doctors were soon on the spot and all the children seem to have survived. Finally, in July 1910, Councillor William Muskett was hit by a cyclist in South Street. He fell, struck his head and died in hospital the next day.

One of the most extensive fires to occur in Romford broke out late at night in the autumn of 1852. It destroyed the *Lamb Inn* and the buildings between there and North Street. The fire started in Mr. Fletcher's shop. He was both house furnisher and pawnbroker and his stock was very inflammable. There must have been chaos as the poor of the town crowded to the scene of the blaze to try to rescue their pledged goods! The next morning revealed a sorry mess of half-burnt and soaked mattresses, pillows, carpets, clothing and other bundles piled up on the cobbles or in the gutters.

In 1890 the old Board of Health chose Samuel Davis, a master builder and Company Sergeant Major in the Volunteers, to recruit a more disciplined fire-fighting force. Their choice was wise. Not only did Davis have the premises but he had the men who worked with him and the character and determination to see that his voluntary fire brigade became an efficient force. Improvements were implemented year by year until their finest hour in the First World War when several men were awarded the M.B.E. on behalf of the brigade, after attending a munitions factory which had exploded at Rainham.

Bad flooding affected the old town on many occasions over the centuries. In 1888 stories still circulated in Romford about the floods of the 18th century after the High Street bridge had been rebuilt in 1738 and about the 1841 flood. These were to pale into insignificance by the side of the events of 1/2 August 1888. Cornell records it as follows:

Heavy rains for a fortnight previously had filled all water courses and saturated all ground and culminated on Wednesday evening with an unusually heavy thunderstorm which lasted until past midnight and was accompanied by an increased and copious downpour of heavy rain. The accumulation of the overflow from the various watersheds so raised the already swollen streams, that they overflowed their banks and great destruction of property was caused. The highest flood hitherto known was in 1841. On that occasion the water mark was 15 inches below that obtained by this latest visitation, whilst the damage done by the storm of 1841 was trivial compared with that of 1888. The water rose to the greatest height in the High Street, which was flooded from end to end, North Street, South Street, Eastern, Western and Junction Roads were all under water, whilst Mawney's Estate was like a sea. Almost every house then built was, more or less, under water. As soon as it was light enough to see the extent of the water it was clear that the consequences would be disastrous. From opposite the church as far as one could see the High Street presented all the appearances of a running river. The water reached its highest point about 4 a.m., barrels and other articles from Brooklands and neighbourhood were actually carried by the force of the water right over the parapet of the bridge into the High Street. The Wesleyan Chapel was flooded to a depth of 6 feet and the water carried the heavy organ some distance from its original position. All houses in the High Street were inundated, the water rushing through them like a raging torrent. In the old houses opposite Mawney Road the lower rooms were filled with water to the ceilings. Fortunately no loss of human life occurred but there were many narrow escapes.

Education, Health, Leisure and Sport

Romford's oldest school, the Romford Charity School founded in 1710 at the top end of the market, survived until 1968. The old Georgian building together with the master's house and the Victorian extension were then all sadly demolished to create room for the Mercury Gardens dual carriageway. From 1930 until 1965 this building had been used as the Romford Public Library. Now named St Edward's, the secondary school has moved to London Road and the primary school to Havering Drive.

A unique venture was started by the curate of Romford in 1856. The Rev. W. Skilton persuaded the Eastern Counties Railway Company to provide room for a school at their then rather remote railway factory, Squirrel's Heath. A hamlet of cottages had been built for the railway workers. The school started as one room but eventually occupied two cottages. Until 1888, standards at this school were very low but then improved after the appointment of a new head, Mr. W. G. F. Osman. The school was closed in 1911 and merged with the new Salisbury Road school.

St Andrew's school, London Road, was another Church of England school, opened in 1843 on the 'New Romford' estate and sponsored by the National Schools Society. The complementary British School (for Nonconformists) moved into its premises on the former Barrack ground at Albion Road in 1848.

A sign of Romford's growth was the opening in 1910 of the Romford County High School for Girls in Heath Park Road, an impressive-looking structure which however proved inadequate, as a move to even newer buildings, described by one first-year girl as 'looking like a palace', occurred in 1935. It took another 11 years for the boys' equivalent to the County High to be opened, in 1921 in the old mansion in Upper Brentwood Road known as Hare Hall. This later became the Liberty Grammar School.

Many small private schools existed in the centre of Romford, in earlier years, some with only a handful of pupils. Regent House Academy in the Market Place educated the sons of prosperous tradesmen in the 19th century. Claughton House School in Eastern Road took older girls. Another famous institution was the Miss Hammond's school in Western Road, run by two sisters. Miss Edith Hammond lived on into her nineties in the same house in a Romford that was noisier and less genteel than the one she had formerly known.

In 19th-century Romford proper health care was at first available only for the rich, though doctors often tried to help the children of needy families. By 1910 there was a family practice of Wright, Wright and Wright described as surgeons and with premises in South Street, High Road and Victoria Road. Everyone knew where to find one or the other in case of accident or emergency! Dr. Alfred Wright was also Medical Officer of Health to the Urban and Rural District Councils and certifying factory surgeon. Dr. Sam Wright, on the other hand held the posts of Parochial Medical Officer and vaccinator, No. 2 district, Romford Union Workhouse. Dr. Charles Green of No. 75 South Street and Dr. Harold Upward were also active in errands of mercy.

Hospital treatment in Romford had begun with the creation of the infirmary as an adjunct of the workhouse. As the population grew and ill-health escalated due to poor sanitation in the mid-19th century, the need for better isolation facilities and surgical wards became pressing. The Romford Cottage Hospital was finally opened in 1888 on a site donated by W. Mashiter in Pettits Lane. It provided surgical facilities and nursing, and also some convalescent ward space. It relied on charitable support and was truly a community effort. From the beginning up to November 1912, 2,400 patients were admitted and more than 2,200 discharged either relieved or cured, it was claimed.

In the early years of the 20th century an alternative medical practitioner Mr. J. L. Haga specialised in massage, hydrotherapy and electrical treatment, although he was not formally qualified as a doctor. His services were highly valued by many grateful patients.

For many Romfordians there was little time in the early days for leisure but simple pleasures were appreciated in a less worldly era. Watching the antics of animals and people in the market place was one of these. Children obtained hours of fun from such unsophisticated toys as spinning tops and bowling hoops with a stick. Cycling became a national craze and a foremost leisure pursuit as well as a handy means of transport in the early years of this century. The better off with a pony and trap at their command needed less energy to appreciate the beauties of the rural environment.

In the late 19th century, Wombwell's Menagerie, a kind of mobile zoo, came to the market place every year and exotic animals were displayed in cages next to the farm stock. On the site of the Town Hall was Swan Field, where the public would flock to see pageants and fêtes and also Lord John Sanger's Circus on its visits.

There has always been a tradition of dramatic performance in Romford. In the early days, such shows were staged in barns and other premises specially fitted up for the season. On 3 July 1820 for instance a programme of short pieces was staged 'by desire of a party of gentlemen, for the benefit of Mr. Styles' (an actor) under the heading 'Theatre, Romford'. In 1826, the pupils of Romford Academy which was run by Mr. Delamare, an ancestor of the poet and writer Walter, gave a performance of the beautiful tragedy of Douglas followed by the comedy of Paul Pry, a double bill of a full-length serious play succeeded by a short farce, which imitated the pattern of the professional theatre of the day. In the summer of 1831 a splendid short season of plays was organised for charity by

Mr. J. Macarthy, a pharmacist in the town. This was known as the 'Romford Philanthropic Theatre', and by chance several playbills and the accounts of money spent have survived. Macarthy himself described the performances as an 'amusement in a manner unusually splendid for a barn'. Dresses were hired from Mr. Nathan of London, professional actors joined the amateurs, candles, gas lighting and good seating were installed and it appears that many of the gentry of Romford were involved either as actors or spectators.

Cricket, football, golf and swimming were all popular in Bygone Romford. Cricket in the area has a venerable pedigree in that the eleven from neighbouring Hornchurch in the early 19th century had been able to take on in competition the best teams in the land, such as the M.C.C. in 1831. Between the years 1822 and 1829 Hornchurch was unbeaten. A poster from 1815 advertises a grand return match between 11 gentlemen of the Liberty Club and 11 of Aveley, for the prize of 100 guineas. Romford sides included many from well known local families and a delightful lithograph of mid-19th-century date shows a team sporting high hats in the fashion of the time, with a formally dressed scorer seated on an elegant chair in front of the standing cricketers. This team consists of George Mead, Richard Parker, James Parker, George Taverner, John Day, John Smith, William Busby, Richard Carter, Alfred Harvey, William Spencer, Thomas Bourne, Joseph Hammond, Edward Kimpton, John Clube and W. A. Warwick (the scorer).

Romford Football Club existed before 1883, some of the players winning Essex caps. In 1909 the team was playing on the ground adjoining the station goods yards over which Regarth Avenue and the cinema block were later built. In 1909/10 there were two senior amateur clubs. The first was Romford United which played on the Shoulder of Mutton field, so called because of its shape, opposite the goods yard field and south of Victoria Road. The other club, known as Romford Town F.C., used a field on the same site known as Cosy Corner Field.

Romford swimming baths in Mawney Road were at first known as 'Craig's White Elephant'. But Councillor J. J. Craig, the well known market place shopkeeper and chief supporter of the project, was vindicated quite soon when local people began to realise what an asset to the town the baths were. Opened in 1904, the baths were in the charge of Mr. Charlie Green, a very dedicated superintendent. Together with local schoolteachers such as Arthur Drury from Albert Road and Frank Edwards from the Mawney Road school opposite, Green inculcated the basics of swimming in several generations of children. When they left school they usually returned to join Romford Town Swimming Club and learn life-saving as well as playing in water polo matches or competing in team racing. A Grand Gala took place annually in October and the baths were covered over in the winter months, providing a function hall. Early cinema sessions were held on Saturday mornings for the children. The baths were fed by a well on the site.

Romford Golf Club, unlike the Mawney Road pool, is still in being. When opened in April 1894 both its clubhouse and course were particularly well appointed. Today the course is less rural in appearance, the Gidea Park Estate having sprung up around the edges. The accommodation in the clubhouse was luxurious. A 1910 guide speaks of 'dining, smoking and billiard rooms and ladies' drawing room ... There are also ten bedrooms for the use of members'.

Important Days for the Town

An important day for Romford was the opening of the railway from London in 1839. A stand was erected on the Barrack Field where the Waterloo Road Estate now stands.

Spectators could view the arrival of two trains that had travelled most of the way side by side on the double track. One Romfordian still recalled the occasion vividly, 60 years later. He remembered the imposing appearance of the trains as they moved along the embankment. 'Here, also, streamers were flying from the works, and the cannon announced to the surrounding countryside the appearance of the procession.' There was also a military band and a meal in a marquee for the passengers who proceeded down steps in the railway embankment to the field to join other official guests from Essex and beyond.

Elections were big events in the days before cinema, radio or television were known. Bonfires were lit in the market and successful candidates were carried round the town. Mock mourning cards greeted the unsuccessful candidate, while the successful one printed a commemorative photographic souvenir. At the 1906 election, when Romford had become the largest constituency in the country, Alderman J. H. Bethell, the Liberal, beat his Conservative opponent by nearly 9,000 votes. There were torchlight processions and a melee in the High Street with rotten eggs, oranges and bags of flour thrown to the discomfort of many who had turned out to see the fun.

The people of Romford are lucky that Sir Herbert Raphael did not take umbrage when they twice failed to pick him as their M.P. in the 1892 and 1897 elections, when he stood as Liberal candidate. It is true that on the second occasion he was only narrowly defeated and he later became M.P. for South Derbyshire from 1906-1918.

On 9 August 1902, Raphael handed over the deed of gift of 15 acres of prettily wooded land plus five acres of lake previously known as Black's Canal to the town. However Raphael Park could not be opened to the public until it had been railed off. The Urban Council subsequently purchased a further 16 acres of park and this was matched by Raphael's final gift of four acres. After the planting of trees, shrubs and flowers, the park looked most attractive. It was finally opened to the public on 2 June 1904. The ceremony at the gates included not only Mr. and Mrs. Raphael and the Chairman of the Council, Mr. J. J. Craig, but also three other important councillors who, when the gates had been opened by Raphael with a gold key, made speeches from a temporary bandstand. Crowds surged through the decorative iron gates to enjoy their new public amenity for the first time.

The carnival procession is a long-established event in Romford, although there appear to have been some breaks in continuity. As a fund raiser for charity, it has always been a firm favourite of the crowds and, for a short period at least, causes a halt to normal traffic along some of the main roads. In late Victorian and Edwardian years a big effort was made by this means to collect money for the Victoria Cottage Hospital which had been established through voluntary donations and gifts. Bicycle carnivals were also popular, with both cycles and riders elaborately decorated.

The most cataclysmic break in the regular pattern of life in Romford occurred in 1914 with the outbreak of the First World War. Everybody's life was affected in some way or another. Troops were installed in many of the public buildings in Romford and the surrounding district. The town was to become as familiar with the sight of military uniforms and activities as it had been in Napoleonic times when there had been a barracks at the west end of town. The parkland belonging to Hare Hall (since built over except for the grounds of the Liberty School) became a hutted military site, occupied by the Artist's Rifles, a glamorous unit which complemented the occupation of the Grey Towers Estate at Hornchurch by the Sportsmen's Battalion. The grounds of the County High School in Heath Park Road were also used by the military. In 1916 it is recorded that a German aeroplane flying over the school caused an anti-aircraft gun in the grounds to open fire, scaring the schoolgirls and the staff more than the plane! Most of the photographs of the town taken during the war years are found to contain at least two soldiers in uniform, evidence of the great mobilisation that had taken place throughout Britain

Beyond the Town

Before the 1920s it was but a short distance to travel in any direction in order to leave Romford's built-up area and find fields, parks and countryside. Romford was surrounded by rural spots, ideal for picnics. Eastwards one could leave the cobbled market plain and travel up the narrower neck of road at the top end. Through the tollgate the fields were visible to the south. A windmill stood opposite Pettit's Lane for many years. It was known as Joslin's mill in 1811 and later as Collier's, matching a mill owned by the same family at the London end of town. Footpaths across the fields here led to Squirrel's Heath. Past the parkland belonging to Gidea Hall on the left, one soon reached the hamlet of Hare Street and Repton's Cottage and the quaint inns, two of which, the *Ship* and the *White Hart*, were of considerable age. From here, the old Roman high road could be followed up to Brentwood and the country lanes beyond. Otherwise, a footpath from Hare Street led uphill through charming fields to Noak Hill or Havering and the view opened out down to the Thames and Kent.

Southwards, below the station in Hornchurch Lane, it was again easy to throw off the dust of Romford and exchange it for that of the country roads beyond Haveringwell and the *Crown Inn*. Where the busy Roneo Corner roadways now stand was peaceful countryside and a watersplash for vehicles. The *Crown* was a country inn and there was a choice of route, east to quaint Hornchurch village, south to Rainham and the bird-haunted marshes or south-east to the pretty village of Dagenham.

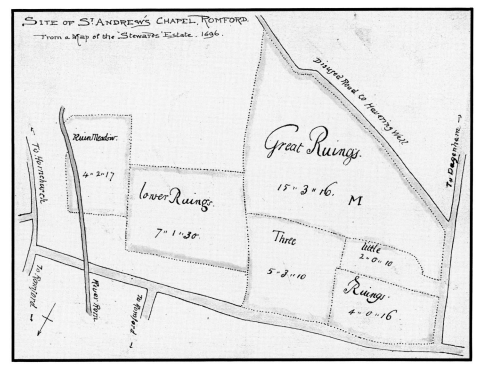

1. A section from the Steward's Manor Estate Plan of 1696 (looking south towards the Thames) reveals how the original medieval site of Romford and its chapel lives on through the field names of the Oldchurch area centuries after its disappearance. Ruin Meadow was, it is thought, the chapel plot, with the rest of the town built over Lower Ruings, Great Ruings and the Three Little Ruings, which were farmland by the time of the survey. Today, Oldchurch Park occupies most of the site while housing hugs the north and west sides. The Rom Valley Way motor route and the Ice Rink have submerged the easternmost meadow and part of its neighbour under concrete, asphalt and steel.

2. Another section of the 1696 plan, differing from modern maps by reason of its south-facing cartography, gives an intriguing glimpse of the layout of the market and South Street areas. The Romford Market excavation of 1984 suggests that the line of buildings at the east end did not appear until the 18th century, as the market extended into this area, previously used as a tannery. The map seems to confirm this. The tannery workings drained into the Loam Pond at the north-east end. The roundabout and underpass at the top of Mercury Gardens now cover the site of the pond.

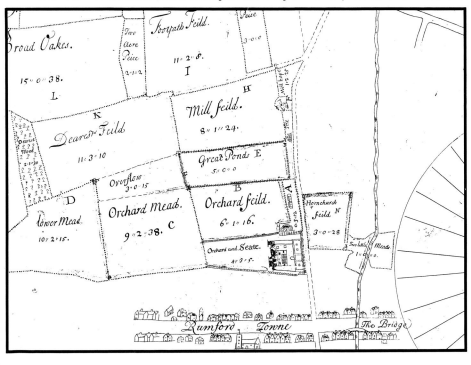

3. Romford's market scenario in the 18th century. Michael Angelo Rooker probably drew this as a stage setting, distorting the perspective and dramatising the height and weight of the architectural features. However the drawing is based on the reality of Romford's wealth of ancient structures, many refronted to suit the current fashion and thus concealing their true age. Known features such as the market cross, the court house and church house are all depicted.

4. This engraving by G. H. Bartlett of 'Rumford Market' in 1831 clearly depicts the classic features that have distinguished this market plain over the centuries. The plaster sign of the *Swan Inn* looks down on horses, sheep, cattle and geese, the old chapel, church house, the court buildings and other ale houses.

𝕸𝖍𝖊𝖗𝖊𝖆𝖘 complaints having been made to the Commissioners for Paving and otherwise improving the Town of Romford, that several of the Inhabitants expose to sale their Goods, Wares, and Merchandize, in the Footways of the Streets, so as to obstruct or incommode the passage of such Footways; and the same being contrary to an Act of Parliament made and passed in the 59th Year of the Reign of His Majesty King George the Third, intituled " An Act for Paving and otherwise improving the Town of Romford, in the Liberty of Havering-atte-Bower, in the County of Essex." THEY DO HEREBY GIVE NO-TICE, that all persons so offending are liable to forfeit and pay, for every such offence, the sum of Five Shillings, exclusive of all other sums imposed by any Act or Acts of Parliament now in force and unrepealed.

The COMMISSIONERS DO ALSO HEREBY GIVE NO-TICE to all the Inhabitants of the said Town, to cause the Footways, before their respective Houses and Buildings, to be swept and cleansed before the hour of ten in the morning of every day, (Sundays excepted), pursuant to the provisions of the said Act; as every person making default therein, is liable to forfeit and pay the sum of Ten Shillings.

And THEY DO HEREBY FURTHER GIVE NOTICE to the Inhabitants of the said Town, not to permit any Swine, Beast, or other Cattle belonging to them, to wander or be in or about any of the Streets, or Public Passages or Places in the said Town, as every person so offending is liable to forfeit and pay the like sum of Ten Shillings: and which penalties will be strictly enforced if any or either of the offences aforesaid are committed after this Notice.

By order of the Commissioners,

WASEY STERRY, CLERK.

Romford, Jan. 10, 1839.

---

5.   The Commissioners for Paving and Lighting were set up under an Act of 1819. They had power to levy rates, not exceeding two shillings in the pound per annum, for paving, lighting, watching and cleansing the town centre. The limits of their jurisdiction were precisely laid down to cover the market place, High Street, South Street and North Street (the last two were known as Hornchurch Lane and Collier Row Lane respectively). The Commissioners' total expenditure in 1848 amounted to £468, of which £108 was used for the 'watching' function, that is, policing the area.

6.   A wealth of detail appears on this early 19th-century plan by Crawter, dated 1812. The long plots run back from the Market Place where frontage is at a premium. In these pre-railway days South Street (Hornchurch Lane) was still a rural backwater. Note the post mill just south of where the railway embankment, station and bridge were soon to be built.

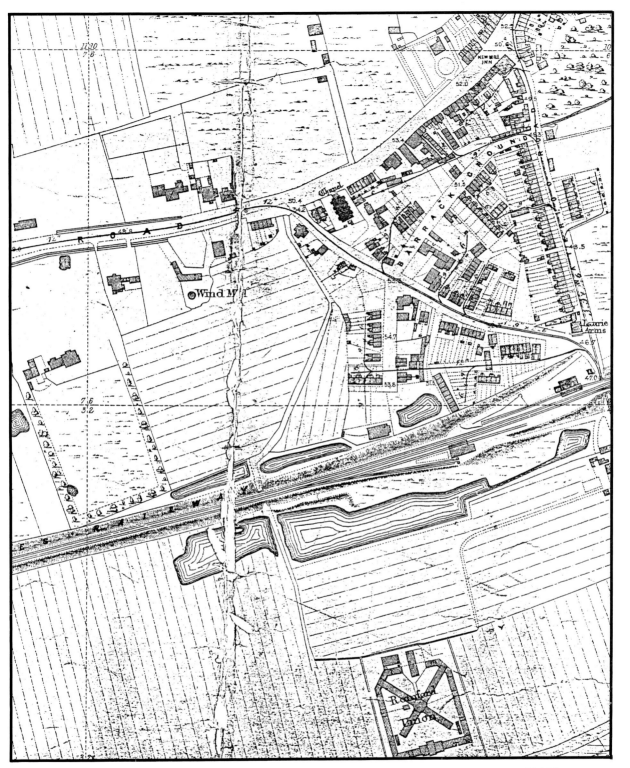

7.   Part of the Gotto Plan drawn up for the local Board of Health. The Cavalry Barracks has become a mid-19th-century housing estate, sometimes described as New Romford. Queen Street is not yet so called, the eastern part on this plan bearing the name 'Barrack Ground'. Nearby the name Waterloo Road (formerly Dog Lane) has appeared, the Salem chapel is clearly marked and, west of New Romford, Collier's Mill is still flourishing in the fields. Large pools of water are shown to the north and south of the railway, perhaps because the new embankment has affected the drainage. At the bottom, surrounded by open ground, is the Romford Union Workhouse.

8.   The central Romford section of Gotto's Plan, 1848. On the left-hand side stands the manor house of Mawneys with the remains of its moat and, above it, a feed channel from the river Rom. On the other side of the Rom is a slip of land opposite Church Lane which may represent the access into North Street of the old cartway across the fields. The owners of Marks Manor House would have driven in their splendid coaches through this open country to St Edward's church for divine service. The Laurie Square and Hall are featured on the plan at the eastern edge. The former is still named St Edward's Square at this early date and retains part of the Loam Pond.

9. This aerial view of the church end of the market place in 1926 gives a fascinating glimpse of the areas north and south of the market. It reveals the first fields only a short distance to the north and also a veritable warren of yards, alleys and houses on both sides, but particularly southwards. Even people who knew the town well were unaware of the extent of this 'secret Romford'.

10. Aerial view of the top end of the market in 1926. All the buildings in the top and bottom right-hand corners have disappeared – the four Victorian house blocks on the north side of Laurie Square as well as the Laurie Hall below and the houses on the right-hand side of Park End Road. Below the square, the right-hand block containing the Charity School and the Georgian houses facing the Laurie Hall have been replaced by the pedestrian underpass, Mercury Gardens roadway and Laurie Walk shops. Most of the other houses fronting the market have been rebuilt.

11. Houses at the top of the market in the 1890s. The lower group of four Georgian houses occupies the area known as the Pavement. Shop fronts were soon to be built on to three of these houses. The top one of the group remained a house and beyond the porch is the narrow entrance to Mercury Gardens, at this time a footpath through the plant nursery to Western Road, which was closed one day a year to maintain the owner's legal rights. W. H. Young was at Mercury Nurseries in the early years of this century and in the 1920s they were being run by Charles Ives. Above this entrance stone dressings identify the Charity School extension of 1834.

12. The Charity School seen in the early 1930s. The figures of a charity school boy and girl have been removed from their niches above the Georgian doorway. Although the boys' and girls' schools were founded in 1710, this building was not erected until 1728, costing £422. It was in use until 1926 when it was sold to the Romford Urban District Council. In 1930 it became the county branch library. The master's house on the right was once provided with a copper for the master to brew his own beer. A hand water pump used to stand on the site of the telephone box.

13. Looking diagonally across the market in 1907 early on a cattle market day. The top storey of the Laurie Hall was still the Romford Town Mission at that time and the lower part was divided and used partly as a builder's merchant stores, and partly as offices for the cattle salesmen attending the market. The extension to the Charity School can just be seen as well as the Georgian houses, three of which now have shopfronts built in 1904. Notice the trees in Laurie Square on the left and, in the foreground, children in old-style sailor hats.

14. Miss Elverston's fancy draper's shop, No. 106 Market Place, in about 1908. The shop window was lit by a gas fitting outside the window to cut out the risk of a fire in the interior. To the right of the first-floor dummy window a firemark of the Sun insurance company may just be discerned. This dates the fire insurance of the house to the end of the 18th century.

15.   A marvellous view of the shops at Nos. 104-106 Market Place in 1917, with motorcycles outside. No. 108 is still a private house. No. 106 is Harry's Cycle Stores and No. 104 is the Laurie Cigar Stores. At the right, part of No. 102, a shop selling fishing tackle can be glimpsed. Mr. Harry Sibley stands between the shops. His wife Elizabeth is the central figure in the doorway of the cigar stores, flanked by assistants Misses Cooper and Bracket. Two of Harry's five children, Edgar and Connie, stand in front of the cycle stores. The Sibleys came to Romford from Fulham in 1906 and had their first shop in South Street. The rooms behind and over the market shops were occupied as living quarters by members of the Sibley family until 1953.

16a. Typical cast-iron fireplace found in these houses.

16b. The staircases were a generous three feet wide, but had many 'winders'.

17. The *Bull* and the south side of the market with its numerous shops and inns are all frozen in time by a cameraman of the 1880s. The boys are standing by stacked sheep hurdles. C. Peck's shop is next to the *Bull*, and others follow cheek by jowl for the entire length of the pavement. To the right of the lads, behind the railings, is a horse trough with a cast-iron pump next to it, close to the roadway. At the far end, the brewery roofline is particularly conspicuous, riding above the town like the funnels and masts of an ocean liner.

18. Looking west down the market in 1898, with the *Bull Inn* on the left. The attractive combination of Victorian buildings mingled with those from earlier centuries gave Romford market a unique character. The brewery chimneys can be seen rising above the other buildings in the distance. Cast-iron railings, replacing wooden versions, were manufactured by Coleman and Morton of Chelmsford.

19. By the 1890s the *Windmill and Bells* was supplied by Ind Coope brewery. It also advertised McNishs Doctors Special Scotch Whisky and De Kuyper's Gin. The yard of the *Windmill and Bells* housed G. Orrock & Co., horse slaughterers. Craig's premises on the left advertise bedsteads, bedding, carpets and mailcarts on its drawn blinds. On the right Stone's shop not only has the standard overhead blind but also an extra vertical one to protect the goods in the window from the sun.

20. Essex Dining Rooms, 1892, before Stone's took over the premises.

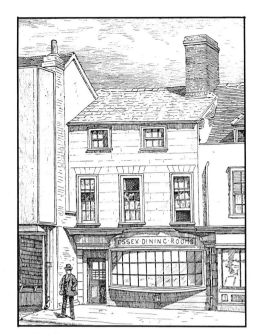

21. Nos. 62 and 60 the Market Place in 1901. Stone's 'established so many years' date was altered each year. The shops at this time were held on lease only and therefore could not be totally rebuilt. Alterations created a warren of connecting stairs and passages. The open windows under the roof remind us that staff lived in until the 1930s. Hunt's shoeing smiths and wheelwrights, a well known Romford business, operated from the yard beyond the archway – a granite block at the entrance prevents damage to the building by cart wheels.

THE HOUSE FOR VALUE.

L. F. STONE,

Market Place, ROMFORD.

Everything for Ladies' Wear.

Everything for Children's Wear.

Everything for the Home.

The Noted House for every class of Household Goods.

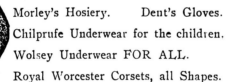

Horrockses Calicoes, Longcloths, Sheetings and Flannelettes.

Witney Blankets, for Single and double beds, Table Damasks, Tea and Glass Cloths, Towellings, Serviettes, etc., etc.

Morley's Hosiery.   Dent's Gloves.

Chilprufe Underwear for the children.

Wolsey Underwear FOR ALL.

Royal Worcester Corsets, all Shapes.

Winter Wraps and Coats for Ladies and Children in Great Variety.

Inexpensive Frocks for all occasions.

Waterproofs and Raincoats. Reliable goods.

The Renowned "Burberry" Coats always in Stock.

The Premier Drapery Stores.

ESTABLISHED 1864.   **TELEPHONE 594.**

22. By 1919 Stone's had become quite a large emporium, with a reputation for value and service. L. F. Stone, son of the founder Mr. Denny Stone, had taken charge in 1902 on his father's retirement. He made a particular point of being in the shop to welcome customers and in this way became one of Romford's best known figures.

23.   The *Swan Inn* had long been one of Romford's most recognisable inns. In the early 19th century it had a large plaster swan hanging over the footway. By the 1890s the inn was 300 years old. On the left was another famous Romford institution, Humphrey's bakery and refreshment rooms which advertised 'Good accommodation for cyclists'. Romford was well placed on the Colchester Road, a favourite route with East London cyclists. Wallis's grocery and provision store, with its display of large biscuit tins with glass lids, can be seen on the right.

24.   A Bamford sketch of the *Swan Inn* yard, looking out into the market, 1889. There was an extensive range of stabling and outhouses. The rear view of buildings in central Romford was often as picturesque as the front and usually gives a better clue to the age of the building, because most of them had been refronted several times to follow the current fashion. The *Swan* yard was a hive of activity during the coaching era.

25.   A long view up the market from the *Bluchers Head* in the late 1890s. In the First World War this inn was renamed the *Duke of Wellington* to avoid any German association. Horse troughs with the inn's name stood outside all the main market houses. Some of the shops realised the value of signs facing down the market; Humphrey's for instance had the caption 'teas' at two levels to lure customers.

26.   The range of buildings including the *King's Head* inn contained a strange juxtaposition of businesses, unlikely in any other town. On the extreme left Walton's tobacconist's window advertises Taddy and Co.'s Myrtle Grove Tobacco. Next to this is a clothing shop which is more like a very untidy market stall and hard up against this, although really part of the inn premises, is the Romford Fruit Store. McCarthy's, chemist and druggist, on the other side of the inn completes the assortment.

27. In this print, sadly damaged, slightly more of the *King's Arms* can be seen. The building was believed to date from the time of Elizabeth I, whereas the *King's Head* was established in 1714. McCarthy's took it over for their mineral water manufactory. Quite a few glass 'pop' bottles of this make have been dug up in the Romford area, where they were discarded on picnics. Many bore a ¼d (farthing) return deposit embossed on their sides. The *King's Arms* lost its licence in 1889.

28. One of the invaluable drawings by Bennett Bamford recording the *King's Arms* yard in 1887 before it disappeared. Some years before this Henry Mayhew in his famous work *London Labour and the London Poor* described the *Arms* in 1850 as the first house of call from London for beggars known as patterers (story-tellers) travelling on a customary circuit of places from London to Birmingham. It was a form of low lodging. Although this particular house is described as 'respectable', there were probably not enough beds to avoid multiple occupation.

29. The back of London House shows a many-faceted roofline of surprising complexity. Notable are the high stacks at the side and the way the building, of Elizabethan origin, grew piecemeal, extending backwards over what may originally have been gardens.

30. This 1877 drawing of the passageway behind the court house depicts the house once used as the *Three Crowns Inn*. The house had been demolished by the time the print was published in the 1880s. The building probably dated to the 16th century. Beyond the figure of a girl, the backs of houses in South Street are seen and an old accessway ran between this house and their backyards, leading to further houses tucked away behind the main streets.

31. The court house looked like this during the early 19th century, when the arcades under the first floor were open to the road. The gaol was on the right-hand side. Next to it a double shop extended to the corner of South Street. The site is now part of the market roadway and pedestrian walkway at the far end of the market.

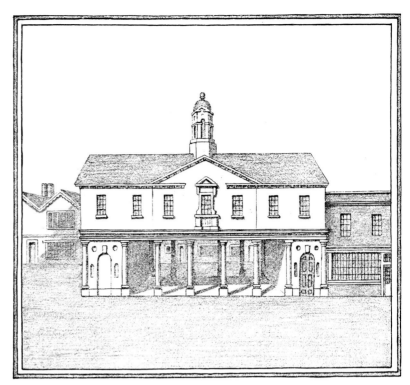

32. This 1890 photograph shows the reconstructed court house, but still with the two shops beyond and the same basic structure. The building behind has been demolished and has left a vacant space. In the High Street beyond, the bank towers over its neighbours. A crowd of onlookers are completely absorbed by the photographer's activities as they watch from the pavement.

33. A view of the shops adjoining the court house, showing how this block narrowed the entrance into the market. The lady dressed in black and holding her cane contrasts with the retired or otherwise unemployed characters who were often pictured lingering here, thus giving it the nickname of 'Lazy Corner'. The shop on the corner had been Richards and was now Baldwins. The buildings on the left comprised Austin's in the far corner, obscured by the overhead blind, Hill's bank, Norman Halls' ironmonger's shop (soon to be S. W. Adams's), Green's the Grocers and Makins Stores.

34. This view (earlier than plate 33) of the North Street/Market Place corner, now occupied by Lloyd's Bank, shows the shop of W. Taylor, which later became Austin's. There was no pavement on the right-hand side of North Street and pedestrians took their lives in their hands.

THE HOUSE FOR VALUE AND UP-TO-DATE STYLE.

AUSTIN & CO.

(R. C. AUSTIN, Proprietor),

Ladies' and Children's Outfitters.

SPECIAL STYLES AND VALUE IN

CORSETS, COSTUMES, BLOUSES, COATS, COSTUME SKIRTS, COAT FROCKS, Etc.

LONGCLOTH, NAINSOOK & WOVEN UNDERWEAR.

SMART, INEXPENSIVE

MILLINERY

Ready to Wear, and Built to Order.

DRESS MATERIALS

Large and Choice Range to select from.

DRESS-MAKING

Experienced Management. Style and Fit Guaranteed.

Gloves, Hosiery, Neckwear, Laces, Ribbon,

Umbrellas, Furs, Etc.

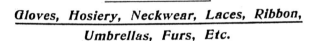

Household Linens, Sheets, Pillow Cases, Embroidered Bedspreads, Printed Bedspreads, Towels (Turkish, White & Brown Huckaback, Etc.), Damask Table-cloths (all sizes & prices), Serviettes (big range), Calicoes, Longcloths, Tarantulles, Nainsooks, Madapolams.

ALL BOUGHT BEFORE THE BIG ADVANCE IN PRICES

EMBROIDERIES.

Very Large and Choice Selection.

All Goods Best Quality Only, at Popular Prices.

R. C. AUSTIN & Co., Market Place & North St., Romford.

35. The exotic world of names long forgotten in the drapery trade is here recalled – Nainsooks and Tarantulles among them. Mr. Austin would lead customers down the length of his shop to the appropriate counter. Instead of a farthing being given as change a customer would be offered a small paper folder printed on one side to resemble a purse, on the other with the name of the shop, containing 42 dressmaker's pins.

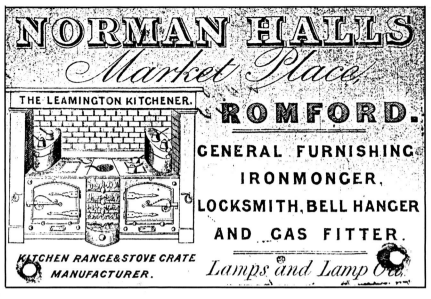

NORMAN HALLS
Market Place,
ROMFORD.

THE LEAMINGTON KITCHENER.

GENERAL FURNISHING
IRONMONGER,
LOCKSMITH, BELL HANGER
AND GAS FITTER.

KITCHEN RANGE & STOVE CRATE
MANUFACTURER.

Lamps and Lamp Oil.

36.   The trade card of Norman Halls, in business in Romford one hundred years ago. His shop was taken over on Halls' retirement in February 1900 by his 23-year-old assistant S. W. Adams and grew to become another of the town's success stories. It gained the reputation in Romford and for miles around for being able to produce any item of ironmongery that could possibly be required. S. W. Adams finally closed only in 1970. This card was preserved, having been turned back to front and used as a label on one of a range of hundreds of drawers along the wall in which small stock was kept.

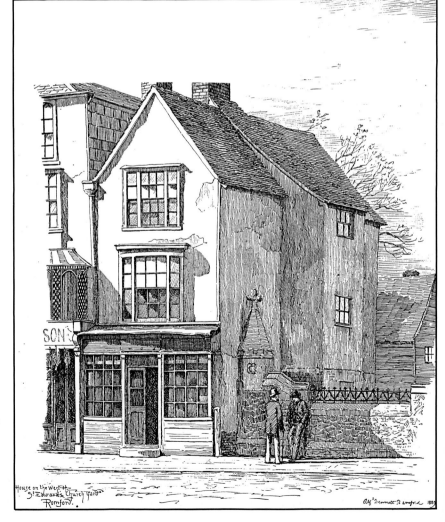

House on the west of
St Edwards Church yard
Romford.

37.   The old house and shop next to the church on the west as it was in 1889. To enter one had to step up, as the floor was on a higher level than the pavement. In other shops in Romford one stepped down to gain entry. The Midland Bank now occupies the site of this house and the shop next door.

38. A print showing the old chapel of St Edward the Confessor before it was taken down in 1847. It features the wooden butchers' shambles, built on the front of the churchyard wall. Slaughtered meat was stored here, often salted down, but with no refrigeration available the meat was often very 'high' when eaten. The shops on the left (west) are typical of the tiny premises in Romford in the 19th century. The barn on the right (east) of the church stands where Wykeham Hall was later erected.

39. Rebuilding has taken place west of the church in this photograph of about 1910. To the east, church house has succeeded the *Cock and Bell Inn*, whose licence has been transferred to the *Parkside* public house in North Street. Joseph Southworth's dining rooms no doubt saw many hearty meals consumed by market workers. The business of J. E. Castle was still a going concern in the late 1960s.

40. Looking north west across the Market Place. This 1880s view shows the *Dolphin*, erected in 1630, and confirms it as a Lacon's Brewery House at this time.

41. One of the few known photographs showing the old *Dolphin* coaching inn which offered extensive accommodation at the rear. It was pulled down in 1900, having stood empty for some time.

42. The north side of Romford Market in about 1900, showing the smart painted sign of Yull the plumber and some cattle already tied to the railings. The headquarters of the A & B companies of the 1st Volunteer Battalion of the Essex Regiment are located in a fine town house behind the trees, believed to have been the residence of Colonel Blood, who lived in the town in disguise.

43. An archway on the left leads to Harrison Barber, horse slaughterers, a firm similar to Orrock's on the other side of the market (*see* plate 19). The next house, the residence of Charles Ellingworth at the time of the photograph (*c.*1910) and used as public dining rooms on market days, had once been the *Queen's Head Inn* according to Cornell. Beyond this, a stucco-faced building announces itself as the Romford Club and Institute.

44. This wide view of the north side of the market, looking east and taken before the First World War, reveals the sheep hurdles in use and also shows the drinking fountain set up in 1885 in memory of Christopher Innes McCarthy, proprietor of the chemist's and mineral water manufactory and one of Romford's best known citizens in the second half of the 19th century.

45. The *Pig in Pound* public house, a particular favourite of the cattlemen, was conveniently close to the market day action at this end of the cobbles. The house was formerly known as the *Queen and Crown*. Two of the market alleys can be seen – one has posters on the corner house, including an advert for Camp Coffee. Further on is Frostick's the chimney sweepers. They occupy the old house which lost its licence as an inn in 1875, the *Drovers Arms*. Beyond is the court known as Ducking Stool Alley. The Loam Pond, beside which the ducking stool was located, originally extended as far as this part of the market.

46. Ducking Stool Alley is in the shadow to the right of Frostick's on the extreme left of the picture. The Victorian houses of Laurie Square in the background loom above the ancient dwellings at this far end of the market. Originally the market ended further west and a tannery was located behind the market frontage in this area. The houses dating from the 18th century were built over the filled-in tannery.

47. A view across to Davey's. The carriage belongs to Mr. Green, later Sir Frederick Green. The coachman is John Barrett and the fine carriage horses were hired from Thomas Tilling Ltd., who also ran horse and motor buses. As was usual in these times Davey's were both builders and undertakers. J. Blackstock (to the right of the picture) is the builder's merchant in the Laurie Hall ground floor. An Edwardian cattle market is in full swing.

A Favourite Corner of Old Romfo

48. As we begin a tour of South Street, a glance back at 'Lazy Corner' with its usual quota of colourful characters and a watchful policeman enables us to forget the frenetic pace of crowded modern Romford. The curious wooden-boarded shop on the corner with blinds close tied to protect the window is at this time the business premises of G. Richards, later to become Baldwins.

49. South Street seems surprisingly narrow in this early photograph. Between the First and Second World Wars the east side was rebuilt further back. The *Fox and Hounds* can be seen on the left; J. W. Braund was the licensee and the brewers were Seabrookes of Grays who owned a large number of houses in southern Essex at the beginning of the century. On the right is Lasham's rebuilt premises. Beyond are some shops and then the post office. In 1912 this was transferred to a newer building, next to the Congregational church, further down South Street.

50. Scruby, provision merchants, with Mr. F. Scruby at the door. He was said to be a very kind natured person. He died in March 1906. He had at one time helped with his uncle's grocery business in the High Street.

51. South Street was beginning to acquire its built-up look, even before the First World War. In this view Lush and Cook, Boot's the Chemist, Sainsbury's and the London and Provincial Bank have all appeared in a row of shops where a few years before there was an empty space. The signwriting on the wall of the old house beyond marks the entry to the stables at the rear of the *White Hart*. The east side of the street has a break in the shops where a walled garden with high trees brings relief from commerce.

52. An Edwardian shopping day at the top end of South Street, approaching the *Golden Lion*. The old houses on the left, converted into shops, are succeeded by the tall commercial buildings ending in the high gabled post office. The pedestrian walking down the middle of the road, talking to the cyclist, has obviously judged the danger from traffic to be minimal!

53. Looking from just above Western Road before 1914. No shops have yet appeared in this area. Part of the Congregational church tower is visible on the right behind the wall and tree next to the five pedestrians. Past Arcade Place, as it is now called, which led to the Carlisle Institute behind the church, two large private houses stand proudly in their gardens. On this site was built the shopping arcade. Beyond, the stepped gables of the police station can be seen.

54. A drawing of the Congregational church. Originally erected in 1877, the first building was destroyed by fire on Easter Sunday 1883. It was rebuilt and reopened by November of the same year. The walls were basically brick, but faced with Kentish ragstone. The two dwellings next to the church on the right were used as a school for boys and then demolished in 1909 so that a new post office could be built.

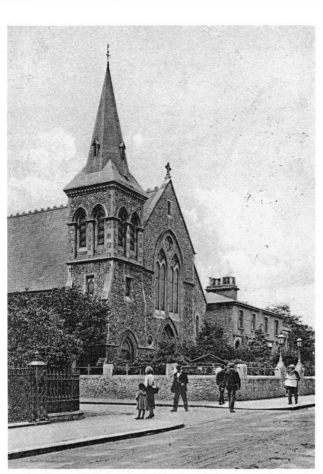

55. Another view of the church corner and the houses to the north in about 1903.

56. The road next to the church led to the Carlisle Institute, the money for the building of which was given by an American wellwisher in memory of Samuel Hanna Carlisle, the eccentric but forceful Romford Congregational Minister from 1827-52. It was used as a Sunday School and Christian Reading Room and later a welfare mission to troops in the 1914-18 war.

57.   Copsey's removal van in Eastern Road. This famous Romford business still exists. At the time of the photograph the firm was very much a family business and Fred and George Copsey stand proudly by their horse-drawn pantechnicon.

58. A good view of the range of shops near Muskett's, probably taken during the 1914-18 war. A branch of the Stratford Co-op is the second shop on the right, followed by the entrance to Wright's studio, H. E. Smith, the stationer, and Daldy's coal order office. The range is followed by the County Court building, and then trees in private gardens. Two soldiers stand some way along the left-hand pavement. Beyond them a hurdy-gurdy man stands with his machine in the road. An impressive official-looking car waits outside the court, possibly for a judge or a doctor. The decorative feature above the right-hand shops is inscribed 'Broadway House 1904'.

59. The shops in this 1914 scene of South Street were built by 1905, and face residential properties across the road. The brick pillar at the end of the police station frontage is just visible on the right. A range of shops topped by a mini-colonnade runs down towards the station. H. W. Hole was a leading councillor and J.P. Further along is one of Romford's myriad cycle shops and a bell symbol on a metal plate by the World's Stores indicates the availability of a telephone, something of a novelty at this period.

60. Another tranquil moment, looking along South Street in the opposite direction. A hand delivery cart stands outside the nearest shop on the right (Muskett's). Beyond is Wright's photographic studio and yet another cycle shop. Putting the view in its correct historical perspective is the sign advertising Collins Agency for Servants. On the left-hand corner is the Gas Showroom, which eventually moved to new premises on the corner of Eastern Road.

61. Victoria Road on the far side of the station led up to the high ground and new residential area of Heath Park and Squirrel's Heath. This photograph, c.1895, was taken some way along the road from the South Street intersection and near Alfred James Rayment's shop. The inn sign of the *Royal Oak* can be seen in the distance. This has only been demolished in recent times.

62. A view of other shops on the far side of the road, c.1908.

63. Miss Dodwell's grocer's and baker's shop en fête, 1895. Miss Dodwell may be the businesslike lady standing outside the shop which is advertising tea, butter, currants and dried peel.

64.   The Victorian and Edwardian houses of Heath Park Road march away to Squirrel's Heath and the 'Drill' crossroads. Around the houses there are still many wooden fences, although masonry walls are also beginning to appear.

65.   The rural backwater that was Rush Green Road near the present Roneo Corner. Vehicles had no choice but to ford the stream. Now this area has its own complicated one-way road system and a mini dual-carriageway.

LA SORTIE DE LA REYNE ACOMPAIGNE DV ROY DE LA GRANDE BRETAIGNE SON BEAV FILS DV CHATEAV DE GIDDE HALLE.

66. Mary of Medici, leaving Gidea Hall for London in a coach, 1639. The Queen Mother of France had spent the night at the Hall on her way from Harwich to see her daughter, Charles I's Queen.

67. An early photograph of the toll-gate before it was demolished. The high road leads straight out into the country road beyond. On the left is the Laurie Hall, telescoped into its companion on the other side of Laurie Square, the St Edward's Hall which was pulled down after 1864. Small gates on either side of the main toll-gate allow pedestrians in and out.

68. This toll-bar ticket dating from 1858, not long before the previous photograph was taken, mentions three gates in the Romford area for which the toll has been commuted by a single payment at the Globe Bar near London. Putwell bridge toll-house was removed only when the Brentwood bypass was built, and originally stood at the foot of the long climb up into Brentwood. The London to Colchester Turnpike Road Trust, the first in Essex, was set up in about 1700 to administer the roads more efficiently and provide for maintenance and remodelling of the old routes. From 1721, the road came under the Middlesex and Essex Turnpike Trust.

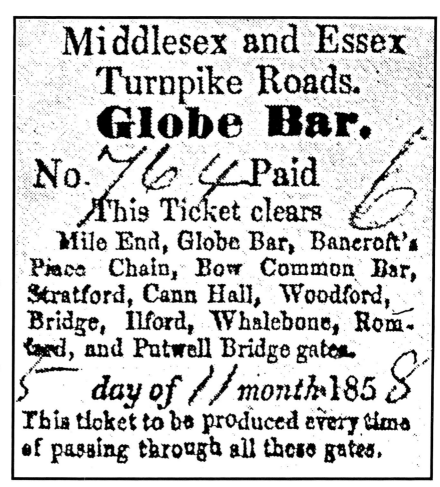

Middlesex and Essex Turnpike Roads.
Globe Bar.

No. 76 ¼ Paid

This Ticket clears

Mile End, Globe Bar, Bancroft's Place Chain, Bow Common Bar, Stratford, Cann Hall, Woodford, Bridge, Ilford, Whalebone, Romford, and Putwell Bridge gates.

day of 11 month 1858

This ticket to be produced every time of passing through all these gates.

William Stephenson,

(LATE GUIVER,)

ROMFORD CARRIER,

To all parts of London,

Through Chadwell, Ilford and Stratford, every Tuesday, Thursday, and Saturday Mornings, at Six o'Clock ; and returns from thence on the same days at Twelve o'Clock.

Parcels may be booked at the Saracen's Head, Snow Hill ; Magpie and Stump, Newgate Street ; Bull's Head, Bread Street, Cheapside ; King's Arms, Bishopsgate Street ; King's Arms, Leadenhall Street ; Lion and Eagle, Whitechapel ; and at his Residence, opposite the Workhouse, Collier-Row Lane, Romford, Essex.

G. I   Romford.

69. This trade card reminds us that Romford had several carriers who would take any reasonable item of freight to London and places in the vicinity. Of particular interest is William Stephenson's address, 'Opposite the workhouse, Collier Row Lane', that is North Street near Como Street. The North Street workhouse was pulled down in 1840. In 1823 two carriers took loads to London the slow way. Malen Sitch's 'wagon' ran from his house in the High Street on Monday, Tuesday, Wednesday and Friday. John Mumford's wagon went from the High Street on Tuesday, Thursday and Saturday. As late as 1910 Mrs. S. Hoppe of a well-established firm advertised herself as the 'original carrier' for points to London daily.

70. An early engraving of the station from the north side, from a note paper heading. The wooden buildings were located halfway along the embankment, towards Dog Lane (now Waterloo Road). The covered way leading up to the embankment was replaced by long slopes, bringing passengers gradually down the length of the bank into South Street.

71. The early wooden station from the fields to the south, near to where the coal sidings and goods yard were later constructed. This station became very dilapidated and numerous complaints were made about its condition. Originally it was necessary to walk across the line to get to the 'up' side for London.

72.   A view from the railway station
embankment in the early days. Romford was
fortunate in having a station so near the
town. The station certainly had the effect of
converting South Street from a quiet lane
into a main thoroughfare with important
buildings. Looking at this print, we can feel
some of the pioneering spirit of the town
which welcomed the railway. The brewery
seems to be working at full production in the
background, and the county court in South
Street can be seen.

73. Inside the Great Eastern Railway factory at Squirrel's Heath, originally the repair works. The area is a store for railway equipment – dozens of watering cans hang from the rafters overhead. The repair-shop function was transferred to Stratford very early, between 1845 and 1848. After this the factory became a workshop making such items as wagon covers and sacks.

74. The clock room at the factory where all kinds of railway timepieces were mended or adjusted. Time had of course a vital significance in railway operation. Frank McKenna in his book *The Railway Workers* mentions the phrase 'the unforgiving minute'. Locomotive drivers and firemen could never afford to be even this late without losing their wages for that shift. The train had to move off absolutely punctually whether the rostered men were there or not.

75.   By the time this picture was taken in the late 19th century the railway embankment had acquired its access slope and the station had been improved. The trees were beginning to grow and also the trade in horse cab customers.

76.   The platforms of the rebuilt station were more civilised and commodious, although until the 1930s there was only one track each way through Romford. Here, a London-bound train steams in to pick up a mixed group of travellers in front of an advertisement for Maple's 'house furnishers of London'. Two huge milk churns await return on the 'country' platform.

77.   This interesting view of the platforms has a summer Bank Holiday air about it.

78. A No. 26 'General' bus, en route to Brentwood, has stopped on the wrong side of the road. It appears to be waiting for a broken-down car to be pulled to the side of the road. The bus has just reached Black's Bridge, by the entrance to Raphael's Park. Lodge Farm on the left has not yet become a park. The overhead telephone wires and the scruffy posters on a makeshift hoarding rather spoil the attractive surroundings in this mid-twenties shot. The No. 26 had at first run from Stratford to Romford. The extension to Brentwood came in 1921.

79. A few years later a covered-top bus on the same route stands in Romford Market. Further down the roadway is an open-top vehicle. Bus services flourished in Romford during the 1920s. There were bus routes from Romford to Brentwood, Rainham, Stapleford Abbots, Aveley, Grays and Marylebone Station. 'Pirate' buses such as those run by 'Chadwell', 'B.B.P.' and 'Reliance' companies also shadowed the 'General' routes trying to steal their traffic.

80. The road to Havering village and Collier Row starts at the *Golden Lion* crossroads. The *Lion*, seen on the left, dates to 1440 or earlier and the first steps northward follow its outbuildings as they succeed one another along the line of the railed footway. In spite of the dangers, some pedestrians still walked alongside Austin's shop on the right where there was no pavement. However in this picture there is obviously little imminent danger from fast vehicles.

81.   The left-hand side of North Street, recorded by Bamford in 1889. Looking back towards the *Golden Lion*, the artist has captured an impression of old houses from various centuries. The range of houses in the middle, though converted at this time into four dwellings, was originally one house, occupied in the 16th and 17th centuries by a wealthy and important family in the town, the Graftons, who also owned other property in Romford.

82.   Further up the street and nearly opposite Church Lane, where the ring road now crosses, was this gabled house, once the residence of the Rev. Samuel Hanna Carlisle, Romford's eccentric independent minister, who wrote a book *Nimshi* that was so abstruse, it was claimed it would be necessary for Carlisle to travel round with it to explain the meaning. This atmospheric view, with its onlookers, has imperfections due to the age of the glass plate negative.

83. The Familiarum, one of the most interesting old buildings in Romford. Sometimes known as 'Canons', it stood to the south of Church Lane. The building was obviously of great age when this drawing from the garden front was made. It is believed that when royalty were in occupation at Havering Palace, the overflow of the retinue and palace servants was housed here. By the late 19th and early 20th centuries the house was divided and used as two dwellings. It is recorded, however, that much of the original structure survived behind the refronting and exterior alterations.

84. The Roger Reede almshouses remained on their 1452 site for many centuries, built around their donor's own home, Joy's Mead. A drawing shows a pump in the middle of the front court. It seems likely the man with the buckets may have filled them from this source. The new almshouses, a stone's throw away in Church Lane, certainly have their own running water.

mford, The Old Almshouses.

85.   Romford Carriage Works in about 1907. They claimed to manufacture motor cars though only horse-drawn vehicles can be seen in this postcard. Once past the works in North Street, above Church Lane, the trees of the Marshalls Park Estate would come into view and the remainder of the route to Havering or Collier Row would be between hedges on a country road.

86.   Stickleback Lane led off North Street on the left-hand side past Como Street – it was a favourite haunt of children as it crossed the Rom stream on a rickety wooden footbridge. These children knew it as Tiddlebrat Lane and fished in the stream or just played with boats using bits of twig or wood. On the far side was Brooklands house and farm.

87.   A cottage in Hainault Road in 1893. This area was considered the back of beyond by those who lived in the town, right through to the 1920s. The coming of the arterial road (Eastern Avenue) in 1926 altered the rural nature of the area and brought development.

88.   Bamford drew this representation of the Manor House, with its entrance via a bridge over the remains of the moat, in 1890. Development was soon to overtake the fields and footpaths of the Mawneys Estate.

89.   A nostalgic view of men clearing the moat on the east side of Mawneys in 1883. Linden Street later occupied the site. Frank Mundy holds a net on the left and Tom Anderson is using the poled implement next to him. Arthur Rawlings, J. Jones and H. Poston make up the group of workers in the moat.

90. The ancient route into Mawneys from the High Street was in 1896 lined with Essex-style timber-fronted houses. Their disappearance represents a sad loss.

91. Opposite the *Golden Lion* on the corner of South Street and High Street was Lasham's the chemist, housed in old premises, formerly the *Crown Inn*. The part facing South Street was used by the firm of Wedlake and Dendy as an agricultural implement stores, conveniently close to the market. Lasham had a new architect-designed building erected about 1885.

92. Taken in about 1910, this view of the High Street takes in Lasham's rebuilt chemist's shop, advertising shaving downstairs at 1d. The London, County and Westminster Bank occupied the tall building and the extremely ancient building beyond, which survived till the 1950s, housed Wilson and Whitworth's Steam Press, printers of the *Romford Times* newspaper.

93. A view from the High Street's northern pavement in the 1890s reveals the *White Hart Hotel* with the carved sign of a hart fixed to the wall, rather than the later swinging, painted one. The pair of houses between the inn and the flat brick arches of the brewery are interesting. The sideways steps up to the front doors were once common in Essex, allowing room for the footpath. The basement storeys must have suffered severely when the Rom flooded.

94.   The Corn Exchange, a privately owned institution, was opened in 1845. Mr. Harvey George, the proprietor, is supposed to have converted it from an existing bank building, next to the *Golden Lion*. St Edward's church held services here during its rebuilding in 1848-9. The exchange was enlarged in 1861 by the owners of the time, John and Frederick Wallen. The corn and other commodity traders came into their own on market days. The building contained offices for businessmen, and public meetings and concerts were staged here, mostly in the evenings, thus providing an additional hall for the town. In 1905, for instance, the Third Grand Concert of the Romford Musical Society took place at the exchange on Tuesday 2 May, the doors opening at 7.30 p.m.

95.   An early view of Romford High Street, looking strangely peaceful as if during an English siesta. Robinson's fancy goods repository can be seen on the left. An account of the 1888 flood was published by this firm, with details of the losses sustained by traders. Beyond is the London and County Bank, before it moved across the street. Richard Havers was the manager in 1848. A barrel rests against the opposite kerb outside the *White Hart* which advertises its livery stable accommodation.

96.   By 1910 the *White Hart* had been rebuilt, now a taller building with a hanging sign suspended from the top storey. Freeman, Hardy and Willis have moved into No. 24 High Street, 'Motors' are advertised from signboards and the pace of life has speeded up a little.

97. The High Street bridge from the River Rom in 1889. The Victorian brewery with its large windows contrasts with the older structures on the right. The bridge probably replaced a ford at a very early date, the land on either bank having been built up artificially.

98. A view from the Rom Bridge before much of the river disappeared under new development. Although a comparatively modern picture, it shows the complicated network of buildings at different levels that had grown up over hundreds of years. Sadly, this view has now been lost.

99. A muddy day in the High Street in the 1890s. The *Coach and Bell Inn* was removed in the 1950s. The archway into
the capacious yard is filled by what looks like a group of brewery clerks from across the road. A policeman stands apart
at the edge of the pavement. Surprisingly, in view of its position opposite the brewery, the inn was not an Ind Coope house.
The street drops quite steeply from the bridge.

100. The *Coach and Bell* viewed from another angle in April 1895. The shop on the right is a ladies' hairdresser. The man with the bucket is probably carrying water from a standpipe in one of the High Street yards to a house without water.

101. A rare glimpse of backyard Romford in 1895. The less public side of the *Coach and Bell* is a neatly-kept house. Over the top of the roof, to the right, the brewery frontage can be seen.

102. A bird's eye view from the railway embankment takes in the generous 40 acres over which the brewery had spread by the early years of this century. A whole army of workers supplied its demands – not only those who produced the beer, but blacksmiths, coopers, carpenters, draymen, engine-drivers, coppersmiths, plumbers, gasfitters and wheelwrights among them. The two locomotives that transported more than 400 loaded trucks daily were named *Eclipse* and *Oscar*. In the foreground, the Rom flows in its restricted channel out of the brewery grounds.

103.   Frozen in time – the old cottages in the late 1890s, before they were demolished, to be replaced by tall buildings with shops at ground-floor level. G. E. Nunn's shop is on the left. The paper boys of Romford collected their newspapers here for distribution. Beyond the cottages is the Queen's House, so called because Queen Charlotte stayed here for a short time on 8 September 1761 on her way to be married to George III.

104.   Smith and Balderson (High Class Provisions) and H. Prior (Wholesale and Retail Tobacconists) have taken over at two of the new shops, Nos. 25 and 27 High Street, respectively.

105.   This is the shop of Ralph Mauro, hairdresser and tobacconist at No. 59 High Street in 1925. An amazingly symmetrical display of dummy cigarette packets and items of shaving gear is mounted in the window.

106.   Johnny Holliday pursued rather an adventurous career. He had been employed by the brewery, but left Romford in 1898 to try his luck in the Klondyke gold fields with the two Mr. Thompsons. He later returned to the town to open this shop at the bottom of Mawney's Road where it joined the High Street. At various times he was Chairman of the Council and a member of the Fire Brigade.

107.   This flamboyant display was arranged between 1895 and 1900 at Poston's the butcher at No. 54 High Street. Poston's had originally been one of the butcher's firms using the old shambles, in front of St Edward's church – the wooden sheds were used to house carcasses for many years. It is believed that the Poston family were the last to leave the shambles' antiquated sheds before they were demolished in 1860 when the new churchyard wall was built.

108.   These old buildings on the bend of the High Street, seen here in the 1920s, outlasted many of their ancient neighbours, finally succumbing to post-Second World War clearance. The High Street was so full of old buildings in yards and courts, that plans for clearance were drawn up in the 1920s and an Act of Parliament passed for the purpose. In spite of this, a few buildings survived into the 1960s to remind people what Romford had looked like more than a century ago. Mapson's the watchmaker, nearest the camera, are still in business, not now at No. 74 High Street but at Chadwell Heath. Axons at No. 76 were famed far and wide for their pork sausages.

Romford, Brazier's Yard.

109.   Families like those standing in front of Brazier's Yard survived very bad housing and health conditions on very small incomes. Their own tenacity and ingenuity, together with a community spirit and a little welcome help from voluntary agencies, enabled them to cling to a precarious respectability. Conditions had improved since the General Board of Health report had indicted Ray Square, as it was then known, for its open cesspool and susceptibility to cholera. Many of the dwellings were later demolished and a Mission operated from three old houses converted into halls, providing a temperance club for the men of the area and helping the needy.

110. The *Sun Inn* building at No. 47 London Road, still flourishing in the 1890s, had stood on the same site since 1632 and much of the building shown was original. It is mentioned in the parish registers in 1650 and 1667. A farthing copper token was issued by the licensee, John Jefferson, in 1657 and one of these was recently dug up at Cranham. The landlord at the time of this illustration was Frederick Charles Ottley.

111.   The yellow brick Salem chapel, in about 1895. Opened in 1847, it succeeded a smaller chapel built on part of the Old Barrack Ground estate in 1840, although the members had worshipped together in temporary premises even before this. The newer chapel seen here cost £900 and adjoined the earlier building. Behind it was the 'New Romford' development built over the site of the former cavalry barracks and started about 1840.

112.   A peaceful scene in St Andrew's Road in 1866. Nearly the whole length is visible, but St Andrew's school is out of sight to the right and behind the photographer. There is a strange absence of activity on the street. The Barrack Ground development still looks new, parts of it being only 20 years old.

113. At the junction of St Andrew's Road with Queen Street, looking towards London Road. St Andrew's church still appears very new in its angled corner in New Romford. On the far left, the houses of Cotleigh Road can be seen. St Andrew's, the daughter church of St Edward's, was constructed in 1862 and, though serving what is basically a working class area, became well patronised by eminent local residents. These included the Coope family, the Inds, the Mashiters and Messrs. Matthew and Helme. The brewery families as employers presumably saw the church as vital to the spiritual and moral welfare of their workers.

114. Street life in Waterloo Road after the New Romford development had matured, c.1900. Queen Street leads away on the left. In the middle distance is the *Liberty Arms*, a small public house frequented by the artisan class. Waterloo Road was not lined completely by houses on the eastern side, although the photograph might give that impression. Beyond the slight bend in the mid-distance there was considerable open ground, used for sports activities. Off the picture to the right was more open ground in front of the brewery.

115. Yew Tree Cottage, London Road, *c.*1860, a
splendid villa on the western edge of Romford.
Beyond there were only a few scattered buildings.
Both the cottage and its neighbouring house appear
to be of solid workmanship. Today Yew Tree
Cottage is occupied by Eric Todd, funeral director.

116. High tide receding from the High Street,
August 1888.

117.   Contemporary magazine illustration, revealing the drama during and after the great flood. The top panel shows the brave rescuer of horses from a yard behind the High Street. The next panel shows a steam train stranded on the Romford line, its firebox having been extinguished. Then we see barrels being swept down through Oldchurch on the flooded river on their way to South Hornchurch. Next, is a scene of collapsed buildings in the brewery precincts. The last panel shows the bridge in the High Street, looking along the river after the flood had subsided.

118. Chaos at the brewery buildings, August 1888. Broken carts, wheels and casks together with uprooted trees litter the ground. The inhabitants of South Hornchurch were said to have been the most cheerful people after the disaster. They were able to 'rescue' unbroken barrels full of beer that had journeyed down to them on the floodwater.

119. Another scene of devastation after the wild waters had subsided: a riverside yard behind the High Street, where an outbuilding collapsed.

120.   The brewery fire brigade engine. The 'steamer', by Shand and Mason, was capable of throwing a ton of water a minute through a one-inch nozzle to a height of 80 feet. There were also two manual fire engines. The length of hose available for use was 1,800 feet. The officials in 1910 were J. Packer, superintendent; E. Abrams, captain; H. Dicks, engineer.

121.   The voluntary fire brigade of the Urban District Council outside their station at the bottom of Mawney Road. The officers and crew were mostly employees of Dowsing and Davis, builders and undertakers. Captain Davis also supplied the secretariat – from his own family! The two ladies at the back of the group would normally be on duty to take the calls and summon the men from a special office situated in the house opposite.

122.   Ready for action! The fire brigade members drawn up outside Dowsing and Davis's Yard at the junction of Marks and Mawney Roads together with their equipment and admiring spectators, both adult and juvenile.

123. Children celebrate peace in 1918 outside the factory school. This was located in two cottages in the middle of a terrace of houses, provided for the workers at the Gidea Park railway factory by the Great Eastern Railway Company. The school had by this time been closed for seven years. The children were attending the new Salisbury Road premises, some way away from the terrace where they still lived.

124. St Andrew's School and teaching staff, in about 1900. The school was also known as the London Road National School.

125. The pupils and staff of Albion Street School line up in the background of this view, looking down Queen Street, towards the railway embankment, with the school just visible in the shadow of the bank. The unmade ground and universal paling fences, plus the aprons worn by the children, conjure up the grittiness of 19th-century artisan life, ameliorated by discipline, cleanliness and determination in the face of difficult odds.

126.   A close-up of Albion Street School with its staff correctly attired and very much aware of the camera. Being a teacher was a step on the road to real respectability and not easily equalled in the local community. Albion Street School was later transferred to Mawney Road in new and larger premises in 1896. The Albion Street building was taken over to house the infants' department of St Andrew's School nearby.

127.   Romford County School. This building was opened in September 1910 as a girl's secondary school. Prior to this, since 1906, the girls had occupied temporary premises nearer the centre of Romford. These were in the old Claughton House private school, Eastern Road. The famous first headmistress Frances Bardsley has been commemorated in the title of the present girls' school. Strangely, when this school was opened, there was for some time no public boys' secondary school to complement it.

128.   Mawney Road School, on the new Mawney Estate, was opened on 3 September 1896. It was enlarged in 1907, by which time the public baths had been on the other side of Mawney Road for nearly seven years, providing swimming facilities on the school's doorstep.

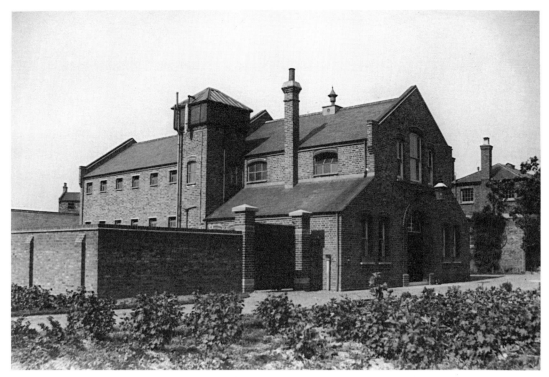

129. Part of the forbidding workhouse buildings of the Romford Union. The 1838 building has survived to the present time. The later medical buildings replaced what was almost a farm settlement – extensive grounds where the workhouse inmates grew sufficient crops to meet their own needs. The Union had a large staff, including its own miller.

130. A view of the growing mass of infirmary buildings in the grounds of the original workhouse, as the end of the 19th century approached. The balconies provided fresh air and open country views in good weather.

131. The guardians and the medical and nursing staff pose outside a newer administrative building at the turn of the century.

132. The Victoria Cottage Hospital with its exotically patterned cast-iron railings, in the 1890s. The hospital was undoubtedly the pride and joy of the local populace, who had subscribed through flag days and carnivals over a period of years to provide a much needed facility. The building was opened on 24 May 1888 and cost a mere £1,000 to construct, the site having been donated by Mr. W. Mashiter. By 1914 the hospital was justifiably described as 'one of the most up-to-date cottage hospitals in the kingdom'.

133. An idyllic snow scene: skaters on the frozen lake of Raphael's Park. Not one house is in sight.

134. Three old Romfordians, 1902. The man with the top hat is Mr. Charles Reynolds who lived where the shopping hall is today, on the north side of the market. Riding in various forms of horse conveyance was a popular leisure activity, at times not without its thrills and spills.

135. Christopher Taffs, 1899. With limited access to other entertainments many people taught themselves to play an instrument, by observation of others and a lot of practice, with sometimes a small amount of instruction from those qualified.

136. The recreation ground was south of Victoria Road and east of South Street (Hornchurch Road) around the turn of the century. Cycling was a popular spectator sport when such a large proportion of the population owned a bicycle.

Romford Harriers' Club
& BRENTWOOD CYCLING CLUB.

EVENING

RACE ⊹ MEETING

AT

Recreation Ground, Romford,

ON THURSDAY, AUGUST 16TH. 1894.

COMMENCING AT 6 P.M.

ADMIT TO ENCLOSURE, SIXPENCE.   NO. 4

137. Romford Golf Club House. The club was founded in 1894 and at this time occupied 90 acres of Gidea Park. It had the distinction of employing James Braid, a famous player, maker of clubs and designer of courses. The accommodation at the club house was quite sumptuous for its time.

138.   Romford Rambler's Cycling Club Carnival group photograph, 1898. The collecting boxes
are for the Romford Cottage Hospital Fund. The hall looks rather like the drill hall, part of which
still exists at the rear of the Romford Shopping Hall. Bicycle carnivals took place frequently, the
costumes were excellent and the machines were also cleverly decorated. Club runs at weekends were
well attended – cycles were in fact the most common road vehicle in late Victorian times.

139. Romford Swimming Baths, supplied by a deep water well, were opened in 1900 and cost £9,000 to build. In the winter months the pool was decked over, providing a hall for public entertainments. James Craig, a local businessman, donated the Craig medals to schoolchildren who passed a proficiency test. The Romford Town Swimming Club, a widely-known organisation, used the pool as its headquarters from 1902 onwards.

140. Mr. Byford's Orchestra in Marshall's Park, 1890. Surprisingly, the players are mostly women. Marshall's Park is now covered by such streets as Park End Road, Park Drive and Havering Drive. The park was then the grounds of a large private house and must have been opened to the public specially for this event. The Essex Show was held five times in Marshall's Park before housing development began in the mid-1920s.

141. Romford Cricket Club in 1887. A wide variety of headgear is sported by members of the team, officials and umpires. The club played on a field at Mawneys Manor before this was developed for housing. Members of many well-known families played for this team including the family of Clube and Major Raphael.

142. The Laurie cinema at the end of the Market Place in the 1920s. The Laurie Hall had been the venue for readings by Dickens and Thackeray, lectures and other entertainments, before being used as a Catholic Apostolic church, builder's merchant, wine store, Romford Town Mission and offices for market affairs. Colonel Reginald Bromhead, later chief of Gaumont British Pictures, converted the hall into a cinema in 1913. Even before the 'talkies' were introduced, the Laurie, by means of synchronous records, had produced a 'sound picture'. In its latter days the cinema was renamed the 'Vogue'.

LAURIE CINEMA
THE PLACE WHERE EVERYBODY GOES
Market Place ROMFORD.
H. DAVIS.

Monday, Feb. 3rd. ➥ ⭠ FOR 3 DAYS ONLY.

THE GREAT IMPOSTER

A Delightful Harma Photo Play. in 5 parts.

✳ **JUDEX** ✳

4th Episode. THE ROOM OF A THOUSAND SNARES

THURSDAY, FEB. 6TH. FOR 3 DAYS.

HER SILENT SACRIFICE

A Beautiful Gaumont. Photo Play. in 5 parts.

✳ **THE HOUSE OF HATE** ✳

3rd Episode. A WOMANS PERFIDY.

MONDAY. WEDNESDAY. THURSDAY & SATURDAY, continuous Performance Daily from 2.0 till 10.30. TUESDAY & FRIDAY. Continuous performance Open 6. till 10.45

PRICES OF ADMISSION

1/3, 1/-, 8d. and 4d

WILSON AND WHITWORTH LTD. PRINTERS. TORN 142

143. An early programme for silent films at the Laurie cinema. 'The place where everybody goes' was a slogan intended to diminish its rival, the Picture Pavilion in South Street. At this time the manager of the cinema was H. Davis.

144. The Picture Pavilion which stood near to where the Quadrant Arcade is now. After the 1914-18 War, this cinema was renamed the Victory Palace. The whole of this side of South Street was set back in a road-widening scheme of the 1930s and the Victory Palace was the first of Romford's cinemas to be closed. There was however a replacement, opposite the present post office, further down South Street. The Plaza opened on 20 January 1930 with Mr. L. H. Chant as manager.

145. A montage to record A. Money Wigram's success in becoming Romford's M. P. in 1895. He was resident at the Bower House, Crange Tree Hill, and the three lower photographs show the house from different angles.

146. Celebrating the relief of Mafeking in front of the church. It was one of those occasions when a crowd 'just grew', as the whisper went round the town.

147.   The opening of Raphael Park in 1904. On the day of the official opening, crowds streamed up Main Road to see the ceremony. Seen here are Mr. and Mrs. Raphael, members of the local Urban District Council and officers of the local fire brigades.

148.   Decorated floats of great ingenuity attracted local people to Romford Carnival. In 1909, the procession through the streets ended in Swan Meadow where the Town Hall now stands. Today the procession ends in Raphael Park.

149. This view of the entrance to Hare Hall Camp, Main Road, was taken by G. W. Secretan, official regimental photographer to the Artists' Rifles O.T.C. This camp was laid out in the parklands between Main Road and what are now the Liberty school buildings, where the original Hare Hall stood. Houses now cover most of this site.

150. A procession of troops, probably from their 1914-18 War billets in Hare Hall grounds, on its way to the station and ultimately France. Edward Thomas, the poet of the English countryside, was billeted with these troops and while at Hare Hall made map-reading expeditions into the Essex countryside. Several of his poems incorporate the names of local places. Sadly, Thomas was not to return from France alive.

151. A view of the Laurie Hall. Intended as a court house but never used as such, it was probably completed in 1853 as part of the Laurie Town scheme to 'improve' this end of Romford. The hall was actually built over a piece of water known as the Loam Pond on 'brick arches sprung from piling'. In former times this area had a rather dubious reputation, housing a 'rookery' or colony of the poor on the far bank of the pond.

152. Laurie Square, showing the four pairs of tall houses, divided by a short street of smaller villas. The houses, together with the Laurie Hall and St Edward's Hall on the far side, were part of a small town planning scheme which was never completed. The projector, a Scot named John Laurie, lived in the town less than 20 years but the square survived for over a hundred. It now lies beneath the roundabout and pedestrian underpass at the top of Mercury Gardens, and the Central Library is on the site of the eastern block of four tall houses.

153. St Edward's Hall, on the very edge of the town, had only a very short life, from 1852 until about 1865 when it was demolished. St Edward's was intended as a place for meetings and public entertainments. The Swan field, behind it and to the east of the houses, had been the venue for outdoor entertainments through the years and so a hall was built for indoor activities. It was also used by the Parish Vestry as a schoolroom and as headquarters of the Rifle Volunteers.

154. Gidea Hall. The loss of this house in the 1930s struck another blow at Romford's heritage. Although not the prettiest of mansions, it had a fascinating history and the trees in the grounds were always admired by passers-by.

155. At the beginning of Hare Street village, only a short walk from the market, stood this 'cottage' which survived into late Victorian times. It had once been occupied by Humphry Repton, the famous landscape architect who died here in 1818.

156. Hare Street village during the First World War. The *Unicorn* public house in the middle is built up to the edge of the roadway. The *Ship Inn*, nearer the camera, is set back. Curiously the situation is reversed today: while the *Ship* has only a narrow pavement in front, the *Unicorn* has been rebuilt and stands well back from a much widened road. The *Ship* is a genuinely old hostelry and in the coaching era it had a companion, the *White Hart* across the road. This very old building has now been transformed into a wine bar and restaurant.

157.   Leaving Harrison's Nursery in rural north Romford to take plants to Covent Garden Market. The Nursery occupied a generous site in Forest Road. All around were open fields with just a few houses in Forest Road and the scattered hamlet of Collier Row at a little distance.

158.   The rows of glasshouses indicate an impressively large area of cultivation. Two of the houses in Forest Road can be seen in the background.

159. The windpump and shed section of the Nursery. Windpumps were widely used in rural areas.

160. Rural Havering Well at the bottom end of South Street. The *Crown* public house faces down the Rainham Road. At the end of the 19th century a bicycle works was sited just behind the inn, where the Roneo works later grew up. To the right of the picture, taken from the Rainham Road, was 'Haveringwell House'. Here on the Hornchurch Road lived a large family able to field a football team against other local sides entirely composed of members of the family, with the mother playing in goal.

161. The tree-besieged Drill Inn corner at Squirrel's Heath. Where the postman is standing is now part of the shrubbery on the Drill roundabout. The corner behind the postman has been extensively cut back. Down the twisting Slewins Lane, on the right-hand side, past the stream crossing, there were brickworks. Houses have now been built on this undulating ground.

162. Chase Cross Corner near Havering, where the traveller could sit on the verge to rest. Times, however, were about to change – the cast-iron lamp post carries the added designation B175 to the Romford road, indicating an increase in traffic.

163. A pony trap pauses on Wright's Bridge in the Noak Hill countryside in about 1890.

164. A neatly constructed family carriage forms the background to a group of stablemen at Bedfords in the 1890s. It is instructive to see how many staff were required to run such a modest establishment. James Theobald, M.P., lived at the house for some years until his death in 1894. There is no doubt that the dog seen in the picture would have had to earn his living by keeping down vermin.

165. Drake's windmill at the turn of the century. The hay
rick, the smock mill and the farm wagon form a pleasing
group. To the south-west, across the fields, stood the post-
mills of Chadwell Heath.

166. James Cumberland, chimney cleaner of No. 11 London
Road, poses proudly with his immaculate motor bike and
equipage. The side box contains all the rods and brushes for
his trade. A wood slat fence guards the open land behind,
but the motor bike is a symbol of the future importance of
machines.

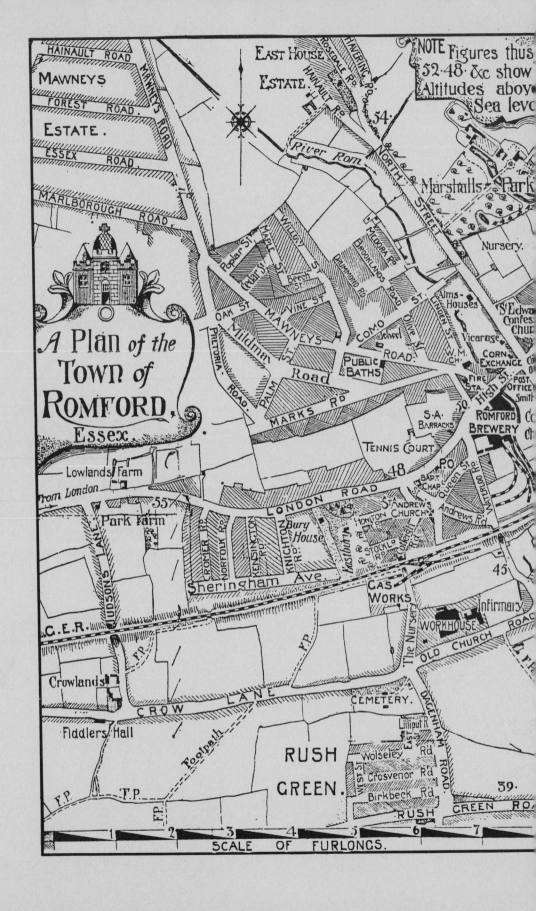

A Plan of the Town of ROMFORD, Essex

NOTE Figures thus 52·48· &c show Altitudes above Sea level

HAINAULT ROAD

MAWNEYS FOREST ROAD ESTATE. ESSEX ROAD

MARLBOROUGH ROAD

MAWNEYS ROAD

EAST HOUSE ESTATE

ROSEDALE Rd.
HAVERING Rd.
HAINAULT Rd.

54

River Rom

NORTH STREET

Marshalls Park

Nursery.

MILDMAY Rd.
BROOKLANDS ROAD
DRUMMOND Rd.
COMO ST.
OLIVE ST.
LINDEN ST.

Alms-Houses

St Edward Confess Church

Vicarage

School W.M. CH.

CORN EXCHANGE

FIRE STA.
POST OFFICE
HIGH St.
Smith

ROMFORD BREWERY

POPLAR St.
CEDAR St.
MAPLE ST.
WILLOW ST.
BEECH St.
VINE ST.

OAK ST.
MAWNEYS ROAD
PALM ST.
MARKS Rd.

PUBLIC BATHS

S.A. BARRACKS

TENNIS COURT

48

PO.
BAPT. CHAP.
Queen St.
WATERLOO Rd.

PRETORIA ROAD
MILDMAY ROAD

from London

Lowlands Farm

Park Farm

55

JUDSON'S LANE

C.E.R.

F.P.

Crowlands

CROW LANE

Fiddlers Hall

Footpath

F.P.
F.P.
F.P.

CROMER Rd.
NORFOLK Rd.
KENSINGTON Rd.
KNIGHTON Rd.

BURY HOUSE

Sheringham Ave.

LONDON ROAD

St ANDREWS CHURCH
HONITON Rd.
STOCKL Rd.
COLLEGE Rd.
Andrews Rd.

Hastbury

GAS WORKS

The Nursery

WORKHOUSE

Infirmary

OLD CHURCH ROAD

CEMETERY.

DAGENHAM ROAD.

45

39

RUSH GREEN.

Lilliput R.
WEST ST.
Wolseley Rd.
Grosvenor Rd.
Birkbeck Rd.
EAST

RUSH GREEN Rd.

SCALE OF FURLONGS.
1 2 3 4 5 6 7